THE GREY QUILL SOCIETY REVIEW

number two
fall • 2018

 MPTF

The Grey Quill Society Review

Number 2 • Fall 2018

Writings from The Grey Quill Society, the MPTF Writers' Workshop

Published by:
The Motion Picture and Television Fund
23388 Mulholland Drive
Woodland Hills, CA 91364

Cover Photo by Christian Joudrey on Unsplash
Layout and Cover Design by Karen Richardson
Interior Background art by Shirley Cohen
Editorial Board: Victoria Bullock, David Kramer, Brent Thomas

ISBN: 978-0-692-15387-1

www.mptf.com

CONTENTS

POETRY

PORTFOLIOS

FOREWORD

What is it about the work in this volume of Grey Quill Society that resonates so forcefully with me? Maybe it's the sheer honesty of the writing, the humor (sometimes dark), the poignancy? Or is it the absolute brilliance of these friends of mine in finding purpose and meaning in their lives through the written word? All I know is that I hear their voices loud and clear in each piece they write, even those voices of our dear colleagues who have passed away since we read their piece in our weekly workshop, and the sound fills me with joy and satisfaction and a sense that memory and emotion sustain us in wonderful and mysterious ways.

I know you will enjoy this writing as well. Even if you don't know these authors, even if you've never heard their voices, shared their life stories, heard them compliment and (sometimes) chide each other, you'll hear authenticity and an honest attempt to share some of the human condition, their human condition, with others.

And how very lucky they are, we all are, that every week since the fall of 2013, Peter Dunne has facilitated the Grey Quill program at MPTF, providing encouragement, enrichment, and most important, friendship to this courageous writing group. Each week, each session, Peter teaches the Grey Quillers more about good writing, honest emotion, the search for the real self, than they might have gotten in a lifetime elsewhere. And this wonderful writing in Number 2 is the result of his alchemy.

George Orwell said "good writing is like a windowpane." I encourage you to gaze through the soulful windows of *The Grey Quill Society Review, Number 2* and savor every moment of it.

—Bob Beitcher
CEO MPTF

FROM THE EDITOR

Remembering Being. Being Remembered.

Each week the members of the Grey Quill Society face some of the most consequential writing they will ever do when they sit down to tell stories from their lives. But their effort is worth every hour. Every word. Contemplating their fascinating (and sometimes dubious) experiences, they have learned to temper their view of the young person they once were with real affection. Not with excuses or exaggeration, but with genuine admiration for the reality they faced and the fights they took on. That is what life is about—those fights—because they are the experiences that develop character.

They know well that every difficult challenge, and every emotion they acted upon in response to it, embedded its moral code in their subconscious. They have been, as we have, unwittingly shaped psychologically and spiritually by these visceral reactions to major events of influence—events of unimaginable heartache, and unexpected bliss—which seemed to have filled their lives.

Refining their short stories, essays, and poetry with this new consciousness, they elevate their work from autobiography to memoir. The difference is important. Autobiography, a search for facts, chronicles the storms we pushed through. Memoir, a search for truth, contemplates the storms that pushed through us. One informs. One forms. One is our battle with the world. One is the battle with our selves. And while there is knowledge in the former, there is wisdom in the latter. And it is this wisdom that distinguishes the voice within each author's articulation on matters of trust, consequence, fairness, affection and loss.

History asks these writers to confront the belligerent ghosts of sins and sorrow, trusting the moment will come in every story when the author's spirit will be illuminated by past events in a new light, and in its shimmer, yield the haunting silhouette of lost hope. From that moment on, personal history becomes a detective story with rescue as its theme.

Week in and week out, these courageous authors become detectives rescuing their own stories . . . rescuing hope. I am happy to report that the child of so long ago is once again the child in each one of them today. I celebrate their grit and accomplishment, and their capacity to still fight those good fights. Their uplifting stories have shown me what it takes to become a brave writer. To become one who trusts the invisible beauty in words—how they work, what they sense that we can't always—to reveal life's most valuable lessons. How to think. How to feel. How to love.

—Peter Dunne
Founding Editor

THE WAY WE WERE

I REALLY LOVED HER

BY DUKE ANDERSON

The first girl I really loved was—oh, well, my mother, of course, but a mother doesn't count. I mean a mother is not really a girl is she? She's, well, a mother.

The first real girl was Susan Stevens. Our house was in Culver City just up the street from the Helms Bakery. Ooh, the great smells that used to come from that place. I was just ten and although I had liked lots of girls before, this time it was real. Susan lived just two doors from me and we used to see each other just about every day. She was eight, but a very mature eight; you would have thought she was nine at least and although I was ten she seemed just right.

She had long hair and it was curled and always smelled like flowers. Her hair was a light brown color, and with my really light blond hair, we looked just fine together. Her older sister Mary Jane, who was also ten was nice too but used to tease me and Susan about being in love, and all that mushy stuff. Mary Jane's birthday was just three days before mine, so she was always telling me how young I was compared to her. Sometimes I would let some of the air out of her bike's tires.

Her family, strangely enough, was a vegetarian family too, as was mine, which was very unusual in those days. They had an Asta Dog, a wire-haired terrier, and raised it as a vegetarian too. I've since heard that's not good for a dog but moved away before I found out if it did any harm to the dog. In fact, we moved soon after I had fallen in love for always with Susan.

We moved to the San Fernando Valley. I met Audrey who lived a few doors down the street, but hard as I tried to fall in love with her, I couldn't. She asked me to be her boyfriend, but I was so skinny and she wasn't at all and we didn't look good together. And she couldn't compare to Susan.

I got through the next few years of grammar school, without a real love in my life, and in the seventh grade, I started high school. It was tough being in high school with all the big kids, but after about a year, I fell in love with Barbara. Barbara Muir. Oh, was she pretty. Lots of the boys were after her, but I was the one she let carry her violin home after school.

On a Saturday afternoon matinée at the El Portal Theater, I had been told by one of Barbara's girlfriends that Barbara liked me. You talk about walking in a cloud! At her house, her mother would let me come in and visit. I think she was checking me out. That's okay. I wanted the mother to like me, too. It was kind of hard walking her home after school. I carried her violin, but I also had to walk my bike with the other hand at the same time. I was lucky I had a racing bike, so it wasn't that heavy, but then I didn't have a hand free to hold hands with Barbara. Barbara attended the same church, St. David's Episcopal Church, so I got to see her there often too. I became very involved with the church and the Young People's Fellowship (YPF). Then a terrible thing happened. Barbara's folks started going to a different church. A different denomination. And they weren't quite as friendly after that. Barbara couldn't see me as often; she oftentimes had other things to do. I was losing the love of my life.

Fortunately, the YPF had elected me president and I noticed how many pretty girls there were in my church. One of them was Carole. She had big dark eyes, and dark black hair, was skinny and was three years younger than I was and thought I was wonderful. I didn't fall in love with her, but I sure liked her. She said it was Barbara's loss. I liked her even more then. Carole and I used to love to dance together. Slow dancing. Really slow dancing.

In the meantime, a girl lived right next to me I hadn't paid much attention too, but I was starting to look at her with different eyes. She was really pretty. A red-haired, freckled-faced charmer. A beautiful slender figure. She was my same age and was in some of my classes at school. Her name was Eileen, and the guy with the arrows was starting to shoot my way. Her bedroom window was opposite my bedroom window and we could sit in our rooms and say "hi" or do homework, or just do what all teenagers since time began do, talk nonstop about nothing specific. I would play my record player loud so she could hear my latest records.

Well, time didn't sit still, and our nation found itself in war, and as soon as I could get permission, I went into the Navy. Eileen and I really enjoyed each other but we hadn't gotten to the level of making any promises about our future. We parted good friends and I went off to save Mom and Apple Pie.

Eileen and I wrote letters to each other every once in a while, and then about a year later, I got leave and came home for a few days. This time, Eileen and I seemed different with each other. Cupid had hit us both, and we were so in love. When I went back to the ship from my leave, we were engaged, and could hardly wait till we could be together forever. The letters went from once in a while to writing just about every day. The letters were filled with plans for our future. Eileen even sent me swatches of material that she was going to use to make the curtains for our honeymoon cottage. She would bake and send me cookies. Time went on, lots of time. I couldn't get home. Wasn't sure I ever would. Nor was she. Every once in a while, the newspapers would report that my ship was sunk. Months went by. I can't say I expected it, but I can't say I was totally surprised. I got a Dear John letter from Eileen. Her uncle had introduced her to his good friend. A marine, who was in town and would be stationed there and would Eileen show him around as a favor?

I was still a teenager.

Well, the war finally ended, I came home and started life again. Eventually, some years later, I found a girl who I loved, who loved me and married me. We still feel that love for each other.

However, I still remember all those girls I was so in love with as a youth. I wonder if any of them still remember me. I wonder.

RHYME, RHYME, THREE FOR A DIME

BY PHIL HABERMAN

A Kaiser roll was only a nickel.
A nickel more a sour pickle.
Toonerville Trolley, a trip to the stars.
With a beer you get pretzels in most New York bars.
Corned beef on rye a buck and a quarter.
A side of fries with every order.
We'd listen to the radio, heard good stories.
Where did they go right after the forties?
Greenwich Village, a place to go.
Guitars and poets put on a show.
George Burns and Gracie, Jack Benny, Dick Tracy.
Daddy Warbucks and Annie, don't forget the dog,
"Arf," goes Sandy.
Ruby Keeler would dance, Dick Powell would sing.
The slats in my bed broke, see you in the spring.
Edgar Bergen had Charlie, Fibber McGee had Molly.
Those were the days, Hello Dolly!
Two Nathan's hot dogs, a potato knish.
Fifteen cents, Boy! What a dish.
Olive oil and garlic, Grapes on the vine.
Firenze, Bologna, a bottle of wine.

Walk Central Park by the light of the moon
Kiss your best girl, the night ends too soon
Snapshots of the past, pictures all gone
They all went away in a flight with the swan
Rhyme, rhyme, three for a dime

"I only got a nickel, Mister."
"That's okay, kid. I'll give you mine.

PEE

BY MAGGIE MALOOLY

L ast night we got in lotsa trouble 'n' it's all Tommy's fault. He woke me up 'n' says, "Skip, I hafta go pee."

'N' I say, "Why you wakin' me up? Jist go pee."

'N' he says, "It's still dark out 'n' I'm a scared to go outside. Come with me."

I say, "No. I'm mad at ya cuz you wouldn't help me get the hen eggs today."

'N' he says, "Please, Skippy, I'm too a scared to go to the outhouse all alone cuz boogiemen'll get me."

I say, "Yer goofy. There's no boogieman outside." But I'm lyin' cuz I'm a scared to go there even when it's daytime cuz ya hafta walk way down the road to a ol' wood shack 'n' when ya close the door it's real dark 'n' there's noisy flies 'n' spiders in big spider webs all over the place 'n' there's a wooden bench with a hole cut out in the middle where you hafta sit to do yer bizniss 'n' I'm a scared there's a dragon down in the hole that will grab me 'n' pull me down in ta the stinky stuff down there.

Tommy keeps whinin' 'n' beggin' me, 'n' I say, "No, Tommy. Go away cuz I'm not goin' with you, Jist go 'n' pee by yerself," 'n' I pull a pillow over my head so I don't hafta hear him.

The next thing I know is I hear Gramma screamin' 'n' I sit up 'n' I see Tommy runnin' like crazy back in ta the bedroom sayin', "Skippy, help me," 'n' he dives under his bed 'n' hides 'n' gramma's stampin' up the attic stairs yellin' fer Tommy. Thin Eileen wakes up from all the hootin' 'n' hollerin' 'n' starts cryin' 'n' Gramma runs in 'n' turns on the lamp 'n' yells, "Where is he? where is he?"

Eileen keeps whalin' 'n' I jist sit there 'n' don't say nothin'.

Gramma looks around 'n' sees Tommy's not anywhere but she usta have kids 'n' she knows where Tommy is 'n' she bends down next to his bed 'n' yells, "Get out here, right now." But Tommy just rolls ta the other side where she can't reach him. She gets up off the floor 'n' runs ta the other side of the bed yellin', "What kind of a boy are you? Peein' out a window! Your pee blew right into my window and all over my face. Now get up out of there and take your punishment." 'n' she keeps runnin' back 'n' forth 'round the bed 'n' Tommy keeps rollin' from one side ta the other one 'n' Eileen keeps bawlin'.

But I'm not worried Gramma'll catch Tommy cuz back home whin my mom tries ta catch us cuz we're bad we jist keep runnin' 'round the dinin' room table 'til she gets tired 'n' gives up 'n' I know Gramma'll git tired 'n' real soon she starts huffin' 'n' puffin' 'n' finally stops 'n' says, "Okay. Okay. But you're going to get punished." 'n' she stamps back down the stairs.

Tommy waits 'til Gramma is down the stairs 'n' sticks his head out from the bed 'n' says, "Is she gone?"

I say, "Yeah," 'n' he comes out 'n' I say, "Yer so stupid. Why din't ya jist go outside the kitchen door 'n' pee there?" He looks at me goofy 'n' then he starts to laugh 'n' we all start laughin' 'til we fall over on the bed from laughin' so hard.

WHAT HAPPENED?

BY DUKE ANDERSON

I was about four years old the first time I ran away from home.

Oh, I lived in a nice home, had a nice family. That was true. I was an only child and learned at an early age to entertain myself much of the time. I did have a couple of children around my age in the neighborhood, but I played a lot at home. Outside in the backyard, where I could make up little roads for my cars and trucks, or in my room where I would make up little games, or read my kiddy books. But many times my playmate was my mother. She was great at making up games for us to play. Easy card games. And hide and seek. It was funny, I could find her easy but she seemed always to have a hard time finding me. She said I was a good hider. Sometime she would go right by me and not even see me if I didn't move. And we would laugh a lot.

One of the favorite things I loved doing was when my mother would set up a lunch on the coffee table and we would pretend we were in a fancy restaurant. She would bring out the nicest napkins and the good plates. I felt so grown up. And we would talk just as though we were real people in a real place.

Or, sometimes she would read to me one of my favorite stories. I really loved those times.

What happened was this.

You know you can push a person just too far. I know mother loved me, but she could sure be mean. I had to eat everything on a plate, even if I didn't like it. I had to brush my teeth, even if they didn't need it. She would wash my hair, even though I knew it would just get dirty as soon as I went outside. She would wash it anyway.

The last straw was her insistence on my taking an afternoon nap.

I had other things to do. I had a lot of playing to do, and naps were for little kids.

So, this time when she told me I had to take a nap, I said, "No! I'm not going to take a nap." I had had it. I told her I am leaving home. And not coming back. I thought that would get her attention. She said, "Oh, you are"? I stomped my foot and said, "Yes."

I figure she would say something about me not leaving, but she said. "Oh, Okay. If you're going to leave, then I had better make you a sandwich you can take with you as you might get hungry." And with this, she went into the kitchen.

Well, this wasn't going at all the way I had intended. Isn't she going to get down on her knees and beg me to stay, I thought? Doesn't she mind if I go?

She called from the kitchen and told me to go get my little suitcase and put in a book and a toy and a clean pair of underwear and socks. She called again and said bring that stuff out to the living room and I'll put your sandwich in there for you.

I was getting a little confused. But I couldn't back down now, could I? No, I'll show her.

She came into the living room put the sandwich in my little suitcase, put that in my hand and led me to the front door, opened it, and turned to me and said, "You keep in touch with us, won't you?" She gave me a little push and closed the door behind me.

Well. What do I do now?

I looked down the walkway and to the sidewalk and to the corner which was just a house away. We lived in a very quiet neighborhood and the cross street had little traffic. So I walked down the walkway, and got to the sidewalk, and started feeling a little funny. But no, I had left. I had to show her. Mother told me years later that she was peeking through the curtains watching my every move, and had her hand on the doorknob and was ready to call out if she saw me starting to cross the street.

I started down the sidewalk to the corner. I got to the corner, stood there looking both ways, and thinking, *What do I do now?*

Where do I go? What have I done? I don't want to leave home and my daddy and my mother. I started getting a little tear in my eye; I didn't want to go, really. The tear was joined by some others.

I turned around, and ran back to the house and knocked on the door. Mother opened it. I dropped the suitcase, threw my arms around her, and by this time I was sobbing and saying, "I don't want to go."

She held me close, and said, "I didn't want you to go, either." I think I felt some tears from her as she held me.

I couldn't quite figure out what happened, but I never left home again.

PIANO

BY MAGGIE MALOOLY

My gramma has a ol' upright piano in the front room 'n' she lets us play it any time we want to 'n' it's lotsa fun cuz we pertend we make music like the people in the movies. My uncle Jim is always sittin' in the front room readin' his cyclepedia tanica 'n' whin he gets tired of listening to us bangin' on the piano 'n' makin' up pertend songs he jist gets up 'n' goes to the kitchen.

One time my aunt Grace taught me 'n' Tommy how to play the "Chopsticks" song. 'N' one time my mom said, "Move over. I'll play a real song for you called 'Blackhawk.'" 'n' she played a song so good we cudn't believe it 'n' we say, "Mom, how do you know that song?"

'N' she sez, "When I was a little girl, your gramma paid a neighbor lady to give me lessons."

Us kids say, "Play some more."

'N' my mom sez, "This is the only one I remember."

So this morning us kids were s'prised when my gramma sez, "Your uncle Heinie and Uncle Roy are coming over today to help George move the piano."

'N' us kids all say, "Where is the piano goin'?"

Gramma sez, "Well the piano just sits there with nobody using it so I decided to give it to a family that needs one for their little girl."

Us kids all say, "Gramma, we play the piano."

'N' gramma sez, "You kids just bang on it 'n' make so much noise your Uncle Jim can't read his encyclopedia in peace. Besides, this little girl takes piano lessons and needs it to practice, so today, out it goes."

Us kids feel so bad we go in ta the front room 'n' bang on the keys fer the last time.

After lunchtime, Heinie 'n' Roy come in ta the back kitchen door 'n' they have some quarts of beer with 'em. Whenever my uncles help move some furniture they always bring lotsa beer to help them do the job.

My gramma sees the bottles 'n' sez, "You better take it easy on the beer because hauling this piano down two flights of stairs is a tough job."

Heinie says, "That's why we need the beer to give us the strength to carry the damn piano down to the back lot."

My gramma looks at 'em 'n' shakes her head 'n' sez, "Well, just make sure you do a good job. I don't want to disappoint this girl and her family."

'N' my uncles say, "No problem, Mag, no problem. Where's the bottle opener?"

'N' my gramma sez, "Where it always is," 'n' she walks out of the kitchen.

Heinie goes to the pantry 'n' gets the bottle opener 'n' opens one quart of beer 'n' pours a big glass of beer for Roy 'n' him 'n' one more for George 'n' he yells, "Hey George, your beer is waiting," 'n' he takes a big gulp of his beer. Then Roy grabs his beer 'n' drinks it down real fast.

George comes in ta the kitchen 'n' sez, "Well, what do we have here?"

'N' Roy smacks his lips 'n' sez, "Nectar of the gods," 'n' takes another gulp.

After they finish their beer us kids follow them in ta the front room 'n' watch them cover the piano with a blanket. Roy sez, "You kids keep out of our way."

George grabs the side of the piano 'n' says, "How many times have we moved this damn piece of junk?"

'N' Roy sez, "Too many. My back's still sore from when we hauled it up here."

George says, "Kids, keep out of the way," 'n' Heinie says, "Okay, lift and pull it away from the wall."

Us kids watch them pull 'n' push to get the piano outta the front room in ta the hallway 'n' they're sweatin' 'n' Heinie sez, "Time to take a break."

'N' they leave the piano 'n' go in ta the kitchen 'n' pour some more beer 'n' talk 'n' laff until my gramma comes in 'n' and sez, "You're spending more time around the bottles than you are around the piano."

'N' my uncles drink up 'n' go back to the hall 'n' start to push 'n' pull the piano to the dining room 'n' they start to yell at us kids again to get outta the way. Then George sez, "My tongue is parched. Need a time out," 'n' the other two say, "Yeah," 'n' us kids go sit down in the dining room while they go get some more booze.

They talk 'n' drink some more 'n' finally come past us to get the piano. Us kids are gittin' tired of waitin' for 'em so Ronnie 'n' Rita leave 'n' go out 'n' wait on the back porch.

When they finally push the piano to the dining room, they're complainin' about which one isn't pushin' hard enough 'n' they decide to stop 'n' git something to drink. They're in the kitchen a long time 'n' Tommy 'n' me go in ta the kitchen to see what they're doin' 'n' George isn't there 'n' Tommy sez, where's uncle George? 'n' Roy says, "Oh, we ran out of beer and George went to get some."

Tommy 'n' me know what that means. It means they are gittin' drunk 'n' my gramma is goin' get real mad at them.

Soon George comes back 'n' they open another quart 'n' take another glass full before they go back to the dining room to move the piano. Then Rita 'n' Ronnie come in from the back porch 'n' say, "When will the piano come out?"

Heinie says, "When we get there, that's when. Go on out. You're getting in our way."

Finally, they git the piano outta the dining room in ta the kitchen but they scratch the whole side of the dining room door when they push it through. They start to roll the piano across the linoleum floor 'n' it's easier but they need another drink before they get to the porch. They finish their drinks 'n' then they all have ta go to the bathroom 'n' Tommy 'n' me are really gittin' bored with them taking so long to get goin'.

At the kitchen back door, they have a lot of trouble lifting the piano over the door stoop and Roy smashes his fingers 'n' sez a bad word 'n' he stops pullin' the piano 'n' sez, "I'm worn out 'n' we still have these two flights of stairs with this damn thing."

Eileen sez, "Uncle Roy said a bad word.

Roy sez, "We should just dump it," 'n' the other two say, "Yeah."

'N' Roy starts to pull the damn thing over to the banister 'n' sez, "Come on, let's get rid of it once 'n' for all."

'N' Heinie 'n' George push the damn thing over ta the banister, lift the damn thing up 'n' throw it over 'n' it crashes down two flights to the cement below 'n' makes a terrible noise. Us kids look over the banister 'n' the damn piano is in a million pieces all over the ground.

Then I kin hear my gramma coming through the kitchen 'n' onto the porch 'n' she yells, "Jaysus, Mary, and Joseph! What was that noise?"

Eileen sez, "They pushed the damn piano over the banister cuz they don't wanna move it iny more."

My gramma looks over the banister 'n' sees the pieces all over 'n' she yells, "Holy God in Heaven, you three buggers are drunk. Now you just clean up that mess and go home." 'N' she goes stampin' in ta the kitchen 'n' dumps the rest of their beer down the sink.

Our uncles stumble down the stairs 'n' start to pick up some of the pieces, 'n' Heinie says, "This is gonna take all day. I've got a better idea," 'n' he takes a lot of newspaper outta the garbage can 'n' puts it under some small pieces of wood 'n' takes a match 'n' sets it on fire.

Roy 'n' George say, "Good idea," 'n' they start to put small splinters on ta the fire until it looks like a bonfire 'n' it gits bigger 'n' bigger 'n' lotsa smoke is goin' up in the air 'n' then we hear a siren 'n' we see a real live fire engine coming down the alley 'n' it stops 'n' firemen jump outta the fire engine 'n' start pullin' a hose off the engine 'n' aim it at the fire 'n' lotsa water shoots out. We never saw a real fire engine before 'n' we start jumpin' up 'n' down cuz it's so much fun.

When we go to bed, us kids all talk about the fire 'n' the firemen 'n' how mad Gramma was at Heinie, Roy, 'n' George 'n' we feel sorry that the little girl wasn't gonna have a piano to play 'n' Tommy sez, "This is the best day we ever had since we left the farm," 'n' we all say, "Yeah!"

DANCING CLASS

BY JOAN TANNEN

O ne of the sacred rites upon entering junior high school was enrolling in Mrs. Cross's social dancing class, at least in White Plains, an upscale suburb of New York. In elementary school, all the little girls attended Lillian Rutherford's tap dancing classes, and we were now progressing to Mrs. Cross's ministrations.

In dancing class, the boys got off easy. They only had to wear their Sunday suits or a jacket and slacks and a tie. The girls were expected to get all gussied up in prom-type formal gowns with all the proper accessories. This edict called for a trip to find a gown that would fit the bill but wouldn't be too expensive.

Mom and I spent one Saturday morning taking the train to Manhattan to explore the lower downtown reaches of the garment district to shop at Kleins or Ohrbachs, which were reputed to have many such gowns at much lower prices than the retail department stores. We arrived at Kleins to find a battleground of fierce Brooklyn and Queens housewives who had the decided advantage of aggressively fending off touchy and feely mashers in crowded subway cars. At the door we were greeted by the sight of filmy tulle and taffeta dresses flying through the air as these mothers simultaneously outfitted their female offspring in party dresses out on the floor (dressing rooms were all full) while clutching at least three other gowns tight in their fists in case the first one didn't work.

Mom and I tried valiantly to grab a dress, but my genteel, schoolteacher mother was no match for these women. Eventually, dispiritedly, we slunk off for home empty-handed. Mom finally found a pleasing dress on sale in one of the department stores. Her best friend Fritz came to the rescue with another formal gown that gave me a change of outfits that her daughter (older than I by three or four years) had outgrown. Finding the proper sandals was a problem too. I had big feet (10 AAA) and shoes that long and narrow were very hard to find.

I was a nervous wreck on the day of the first dancing class. I had set my hair but it was a damp day, and I could never depend on my hair to stay curled. I was bathed and scented and all dressed and ready to go. We didn't have a car at that time so Norma's father was going to drive us to the facility where Mrs. Cross held court. Norma was my best friend. We entered the ballroom and found all the boys sitting on one side of the room and the girls in their finery on the opposite side of the room. The band struck up for the first time. My uncle Ralph ("Count" as he was called) played drums and was the leader of the band. Mrs. Cross gave the signal for the boys to pick a partner. The boys clattered across the floor like a herd of cattle and en masse they headed for the cute, little ones. Finally, they got straightened out and each found a partner. I sat there like a deer caught in the headlights. I was the tallest in my class (5'8") and the boys milled around me but not to me. Mrs. Cross had to separate two boys fighting over one girl, as she handed one of them to me. I was humiliated in front of my uncle up on the bandstand because he was witness to my social deficiencies. I felt like a giraffe next to the young man who was reluctantly paired with me, his sweaty hand awkwardly clutching the back of my dress, his head topping off at about my nose.

I was happy when the evening came to an end, but I was faced with fifty-two more weeks of the same. However, it turned out that it wasn't so bad after all. I was usually picked by somebody to partner with. Needless to say, I was never picked by one of the really cute guys that I secretly lusted after, but I wasn't the dud that I was at the first class. And, I learned how to be a pretty good dancer.

In high school, we met many new people, and we all seemed to fill out and shape up and become fairly normal social beings.

RONNIE

BY MAGGIE MALOOLY

So much happened today I can't stop thinking 'bout it. My mom invited all my aunts 'n' cousins 'n' some of her girlfriends to our apartment cuz today is Ronnie's birthday 'n' it's a special birthday cuz Ronnie is six 'n' he's gonna start first grade. But he can't go to Our Lady of the Angels school like we do 'n' my mom had ta find a special school for him cuz Ronnie can't run anymore 'n' he has ta walk on his toes to keep his balance 'n' he can't get up 'n' down stairs without us helping him.

Last night when we were all in bed Tommy says, "Ronnie are ya scared to go ta different school where ya don't know nobody?"

'N' Ronnie says, "I dunno but it's okay cuz I wanna go ta school,"

'N' Eileen says, "Not me. I don't wanna go on a bus away from home every day."

'N' Tommy says, "You're such a scaredy cat you don't wanna do nothing," 'n' Eileen stuck out her tongue.

This morning after breakfast all us kids had ta help get stuff ready for the party. Eileen 'n' me had the job ta set the dining room table for the grownups 'n' Tommy had the job a put up the card table for all the kids 'n' Rita 'n' Ronnie had the job to stay out of everybody's way 'n' Gramma had ta bake Ronnie's favorite two-layer chocolate cake with lots a chocolate frosting in the middle 'n' lots more on the top.

The party was real fun 'n' Ronnie blew out all the candles on his cake in one breath 'n' he got some good presents for school. He got two pencils, a eraser, a paper tablet, a pencil sharpener, a pair of socks, a brand new shirt for school, 'n' two puzzle games. All us kids said how lucky he was ta get such good stuff.

After the party when all the company was gone, we started ta clean up the mess when the front door opened 'n' my Uncle George walked in ta the hallway. Tommy saw him first 'n' yelled, "Uncle George, you're home!" 'n' all us kids yelled, "Uncle George, Uncle George," 'n' he yelled, "Hi, kids."

'N' we all ran ta him 'n' jumped on him so hard we knocked him over 'n' piled on top of him cuz us kids were so s'prised to see him back home again.

Tommy said, "Are ya gonna stay? 'n' my uncle said, "Yes, I am," 'n' we were so glad he said that cuz we missed him so much.

Dinner was fun tonight 'n' we were all telling Uncle George 'bout the party he missed when he said, "Ronnie, I'm thinking you should have a very special birthday present today. What do you think?"

'N' Ronnie says, "Okay," 'n' Uncle George says, "Let's celebrate. Let's go out to Midway Airport and watch the airplanes take off," 'n' we all yell, "Yeaaaaaa!"

My Uncle George knows a special secret place to watch airplanes take off 'n' he drives all 'round the whole airport 'n' parks at the wire fence that's right at the end of the runway. When it's time for a plane ta take off we can see it move over ta the runway 'n' then start ta move faster 'n' faster 'n' it's two big headlights shine right in ta our car 'n' it comes closer 'n' closer ta us 'n' when it's right in front of us it starts to lift up 'n' up 'n' flies right over our car 'n' the noise is so loud ya think your ears are gonna bust 'n' we all scream 'n' shut our eyes cuz we're so scared it'll crash right in ta us.

It's the bestest fun of anything 'n' afterwards we all laugh 'n' brag who kept their eyes open the longest. We all say I did, I did 'n' we ask Uncle George to tell who was the bravest one who kept their eyes open the longest before the plane flew over us.

My Uncle George looks at us 'n' says, It was Ronnie. He was the bravest 'n' Ronnie laughs 'n' gets a big smile on his face 'n' I think my Uncle George said he was the bravest cuz today is Ronnie's birthday.

❈

This morning my mom woke us all up early cuz it's Ronnie's first day ta go ta the special school for kids who can't go ta a regular school. The bus is gonna pick him up at eight o'clock 'n' my mom has ta help him get dressed before she goes ta work at Mrs. Spiking's office.

I'm happy that Ronnie is going ta school but I'm sad too cuz he's never been away from us before 'n' I hope he'll be safe cuz we always watch over him. He looks real nice cuz my mom put on his new socks, his best knickers 'n' his brand-new birthday shirt. Tommy tied his high-top shoes 'n' my mom combed his hair 'n' he looks real good. Then my mom hugged 'n' kissed Ronnie 'n' said, "Be a good boy," but she is just saying that cuz Ronnie is always a good boy.

When my mom left for work, Gramma says, "I made your favorite breakfast," 'n' we all know it isn't Cream of Wheat cuz Ronnie hates Cream of Wheat 'n' my gramma says, "I made pancakes for you," 'n' Ronnie was glad.

When it was time to go downstairs to get the bus Tommy 'n' me helped Ronnie walk down the stairs so he wouldn't fall 'n' we waited 'til the bus came 'n' Tommy helped him up the bus stairs 'n' got him to his seat 'n' we waved goodbye when it left 'n' Ronnie never cried once.

THE BLUE SWEATER

BY DEBORAH ROGOSIN

It was fun to go to Grandma's house. She always greeted me with a big hug and a smile and everything in her home was so interesting. She lived with my two single aunts, Gerry and June, and my Uncle Mel who was still in high school though they were always at work or at school or football practice.

Once during the 1939 San Francisco World's Fair, my parents went on vacation and left my sister and me there. But probably the most fun I had, if I had a new shiny penny, was skipping a half block to the Mom and Pop Store, Molly's Market nearby or as I called it "The Candy Store."

At times, I couldn't decide if I wanted a piece of bubble gum or a licorice twist. The candy counter had everything, jelly bellies, gumballs, candy corn, jawbreakers, tootsie rolls, gum drops an so much more. For a nickel you could get a big Hershey bar, Milky Way, a Mars Bar, a Big Hunk, a box of Milk Duds, or an Oh Henry! And I was eager to see what "Molly" had in the case.

I would enter the screen door and notice the fan was on. Streamers of flypaper were hanging from the ceiling. It had shelves along the walls, a deli case which contained fresh bakery items baked by Molly, and sliced meats and a variety of cheeses across from the candy. A refrigerated unit in the back left corner had milk and other dairy items, and Coca-Cola. Molly sat behind the candy counter, a small woman but strong and fast moving, she wore her salt and pepper gray hair pulled back, and glasses with a pencil behind her ear, and always wore a smile. Covering her shoulders was a blue sweater. She was quick to jump off her stool and help people find things they needed.

I would check everything out on that tall candy counter and

would go back and look at the pickle barrel, but I never touch anything unless I had money to buy it.

Molly and her husband, Max, had come from the spa country of Germany in 1936 after an incident with some Nazi's. Her father had been mayor of the town but had been fired from office by the SS since he was Jewish. The next day the whole family left, leaving everything behind. They said, "We saw the writing on the wall." They went to night school to learn English, and within a year opened a small store across the street from the Grammar school.

I did visit my grandmother often but when I was in the third grade, we moved a few blocks away. One day, two boys came in and one boy asked Molly where the cream was while the other boy stuffed candy in his pockets. I called Molly and scratched my head and when the boys weren't looking I mouthed "thief" to Molly. She asked them to pay for the candy they had put in their pockets. After that, I hung out after school sometimes and gave Molly a signal when I saw someone stealing something, usually but not always from the candy counter. I lived there for a while but moved to Reno, Nevada for the fourth and fifth grades. We returned on D-Day, June 4, 1944, and again settled nearby Molly's.

As I got older Molly would have me help her make Strudel. She would take out her *volger holtz*, a European version of a rolling pin, throw the dough and roll it oh so thin. Her husband used to say with a laugh, when it's thin enough I'll be able to read the newspaper through it. We would pour jam all over it, smooth it out and then sprinkle it with currants, dried chopped apples, and nuts. Molly would roll it up and bake it and it was so delicious! Molly would make cookies, too, and send me home with the broken ones. Sometimes I saw her break them.

Her teenage son, Herbert, was nice to me and said I was a pretty girl and he was going to marry me when I grew up some more. I thought he was so funny and handsome, too! Molly's husband Max stayed pretty much upstairs in the apartment over the store and made violins.

One day, when I was ten years old, I was skating home across the street on the playground from her store and she ran out and put that blue sweater over my shoulders and said, "Run home quickly before you catch a cold, a storm is moving in."

I kept that sweater and put it over my shoulders when I went to sleep at night. One morning more than a week later, I woke up in my snuggly bed and thought to myself, "Molly must be cold without her sweater!" I returned it that afternoon and apologized for not bringing it back sooner. She said, "It's okay, honey, I knew you'd bring it back. You have so much integrity." I went home and looked it up in the dictionary and felt a special closeness to Molly.

A few months later I noticed she was sometimes wearing her son's navy blue sweater. I asked her why she wasn't wearing her pretty blue sweater. She told me she threw it out since it was old and her son wouldn't need his sweater anymore, because, Herbert, her only child, had been killed in action in France. Tears started rolling down her cheeks and I gave her a hug and started crying, too. He was always so nice to me. He was the first person I knew who died and I was very, very sad. The next time I saw Molly she had a sign in her window that said she was a Gold Star Mother. She tearfully explained to me what that meant.

Through high school, I used to help her out from time to time, doing errands and helping her bake. When I went to the senior prom she made a formal for me. I wore it again at a college dance. Molly was so special to me, and she always made me feel good. She was more like a grandmother than my own grandmothers.

She was a friend and a mentor to me, and someone I will never forget.

She was one of several people who touched my life!

FRAGMENTS

BY JOEL ROGOSIN

I'm thinking of somersaults
and cartwheels
and roller-skates and swings
those few, newly remembered
mostly in the summertime
growing up things
with bare feet kicking pebbles everywhere
and naked arms and legs akimbo in the air
swan diving into pools of sunlit green
hidden in places no one else had ever seen
waiting for somebody, anyone at all
to notice I was there beside
the ivy-covered garden wall
hoping they would see me but not to stare
wanting to belong
not knowing how or where
whispering a comfort song
so high up in a leafy bough
well, maybe not quite that high . . .
I'm turning eighty now
with many memories left to share
perhaps I should be
moving on somewhere
and just get past it all
at last
yet, I think they will keep

and some night
just might
help welcome asleep . . .
I'm thinking of somersaults
and cartwheels
and roller-skates and swings
those few, newly remembered
mostly in the summertime
growing up things

NEVER ENOUGH CATSUP FOR YOUR BAKED BEANS

BY MADI SMITH-LAWRENCE

I keep the assignment in front of me because I don't trust myself to do what's been asked. I have always found it's easier to trust or believe in someone else rather to believe or trust in myself. Maybe because I had never been believed in or trusted as a child. So what. I thought I was a good kid because I was afraid not to be. The threat of being returned to an orphanage was always hanging over my head. My mother would drive me up to the gates of Villa Cabrini and tell me to get out. I'd cry and beg and promise to be a good girl as she drove off. I'm sure she wasn't gone very long, but it seemed like an eternity to me. I did find out later that it wasn't even an orphanage and that I didn't come from an orphanage, not that that was a bad thing, but at the time it was terrifying. I had no idea what I was supposed to do other than stay clean, speak when spoken to and smile no matter what. My mother could go off for no reason at all. No one questioned this. She believed in her power and that was enough for everyone else.

My grandma was my mother's mother. My first memory of her was when I was in my crib. I loved my crib. It made me feel safe. I can still remember the safety and the soft comfort of my grandma's handmade quilts that protected me. I guess I was around two or three. Yes, I can remember back then. She would visit us at our home in Burbank, California where I grew up.

Grandma had a 1937 gray Ford coupe. When she came to visit us she would sneak into my bedroom while I was taking a nap and against my mother's wishes, put her finger to her lips not to make a noise. I can remember her lifting me out of my crib way up in the air and talking to me in soft whispers. She made me feel like I was the most loved and important thing in the whole world. My grandma was my saving grace. She had the patience of Job and with me she needed it. I did try to emulate her, but I didn't always achieve those traits. I think I'm a combination of my mother's impatience with imperfection and my grandma's tenacity, and, I hope kindness, strength, and empathy.

My grandma had the softest white hair that looked like a halo around her head. She had subtle pearl pink skin and I loved to touch the softness of her underarms. What patience she had with me. Though her hands were strong and rugged from hard work, her touch was tender. I can see them now, calloused with blue veins like spiders crisscrossing across the tops. Her face was round and soft with a smile that could melt your heart. She had gray-green eyes with sparks of amber and in her soft-pink ear lobes, tiny antique diamonds. When Grandma came to visit us in Burbank she always wore her navy blue skirt suit, pearls, a white nylon blouse and black leather medium-heeled shoes.

At home on her ranch, where my mother dropped me off every summer, Grandma always wore dresses, and always with an apron wrapped around her. And where, in the apron's pocket, she always kept lemon drops. She would give me her secret wink when it was okay to take one. One of a thousand sweet memories I have of my time living with them.

I grasp the straw broom in my hands. My thoughts drift back to my grandma. I hear her words, "Honey, keep the broom on the ground. Try not to pick it up. If you do, it might move the dust again and then you'd have to do it all over again." She'd smile, grasp the broom in her beautiful gentle hands, never condescending, always respecting my adolescent ego, with intelligence and great love she would demonstrate.

Each time I iron, attach a new button, (I still have her sterling silver thimbles) or make a bed, her presence appears. She was the original domestic goddess. She was always doing. Always giving to others. My grandma could bake, chop wood, kill a rattler with one fell swoop of her garden hoe, do the laundry in a bucket, hang them on a line in the sunshine, create and sew by hand beautiful soft cotton quilts for me, garden, attach a new roof, and always be the perfect, feminine woman. Never too busy to give you her beautiful smile, a hug, prepare your favorite dish, or repair your favorite doll's leg . . . and never ever a thought of herself. She was strong, gentle and ever a female.

Grandma was born Rachel Dawson in Chicago, Illinois. Married Herman Weller, gave birth to my mother and my aunt Jennie, traveled to California on shipboard through the Panama Canal, ran away from Herman because of his abuse, lived happily with Johnny Long until he died, and fell in love with my Grandpa Sug Cromer.

Her little house had no electricity or running water but holds the most warm and beautiful memories in my heart. It was nestled in a little valley covered with live oaks. There was a great barn filled with the aroma of hay, barley, corn, cow and horse manure. To this day I love the smell of manure.

When I was seven or eight, my grandma started teaching me how to cook, crochet, churn butter, milk the cow, and feed the horses and chickens. Entering the barn, I was hit with the heady essence of Dunny, Lucky, and Lucy the cow. Their soft noses, the warm underbelly of Lucy, they still fill my head, nose, and heart. Gathering the eggs from the chicken coop in the barn, I was always surprised to find a newly laid, warm egg in their straw nests. There was a huge tree stump nearby my grandma used for chickens, which I won't elaborate on. Of course, there was an awful outhouse which smelled beyond description.

Her home was only heated by a potbelly stove in the main room. In the kitchen, there was a pump for water and a wood-burning stove for cooking. This was paradise. Two live oaks held a hammock. And on hot summer days was the only cool place to be. Whenever we saw dust coming from the dirt road up the hill she'd say, "Quick, get in the house, the Holy Rollers are coming and I'm too busy for them."

We'd hightail it into the house and hide until we thought they'd give up and leave. But they outwaited her and my grandma would finally give in taking some cookies and freshly squeezed lemonade out to them. We'd sit and listen to their stories. My grandma would wink at me to say, "just be kind and let them say their peace."

At night my grandma would light her kerosene lamps, stoke the fire and bring out her guitar and whistle her favorite tunes. I loved her and those precious summers. My grandma was a treasure.

All of a sudden I'm filled with my grandma's presence. In my mind's eye, she's standing over her wood-burning stove, apron wrapped around her, chopping the kindling to fit into the little round iron holes that she opened with a special hook. Just the smell of wood burning is still heavenly to me. My grandma always whistled as she cooked. In the morning she'd start the stove, pump some water for the coffee. Then peel apples for either applesauce cake or apple pie. She'd make the dough for biscuits and the apple pie crust. I see her hands, gnarled and beautiful. Skillful, covered with flour, gently rolling out the pie crust and kneading the dough for biscuits or bread. My grandma loved pork. On Sundays, we would have pork sausage that she cooked with eggs her hens had laid, butter she churned, honey from her beehives. Ecstasy.

All the priceless gifts my grandma and Grandpa Sug taught me: kindness, tenacity, strength with empathy . . . except for a bag of kittens, but I think that was something my mother made up because I never saw a stream near their property, and besides my grandma would never do anything to harm an animal except when it came to rattlesnakes because they never had a chance with my grandma's hoe. Also, if there had been a stream on their property I would have been in it.

My grandma taught me to love without judgment. She taught me to work hard and feel good about giving to others. Share for its own sake. Give with all your heart and energy, for that is your own reward. It's difficult for me sometimes to live up to her. She was perfect in every way.

Now my Grandpa Sug was a big man, 6′2″ without his boots. Talk about gnarled hands; they were calloused, cracked, like old leather. He was slightly bent from riding the range from daybreak to nightfall. He had strong blue eyes and a full head of steel gray hair. He was a real Texas sheriff who patrolled the Mexico-California border on horseback.

His full name was Grandpa Sug Cromer and boy did I love him. He was a beaut. Everything a hopeful cowgirl of five could ever dream of having. Grandpa Sug was rugged as they came but gentle of heart. He came to California on horseback from Texas and soon met and fell in love with my grandma.

He was a giant and a real cowboy. I guess that's how he captured my grandma's heart. Grandpa Sug worked the local rodeos and rode Brahma Bulls to earn extra money. Looking back I guess it was a hard and simple life, but to me, it was romance personified. They first lived in Brawley, California, on a dusty little ranch. All I remember was the hard pounded dirt of their corral with a barn that filled my heart with such joy.

Grandma would start the day before the sun came up adding kindling from a box next to the potbelly stove, lighting the kerosene lamps and pumping the water for coffee. She'd send me out to the barn to milk the cow and bring in the eggs from the hen house. After breakfast of thick sliced bacon, fresh eggs, and biscuits, Grandpa Sug would sip his coffee, lean back in his chair and say, "Well honey, what do you think we have to do today? Maybe we should take a look at Lucky and see if we can get a bridle on him. What do you think?" He'd smile, lean over and chuck me on the chin. "Come on, let's take a look at Lucky." Grandma would roll her eyes and give me a wink.

We'd go out the kitchen door slamming the screen door behind us. Grandpa Sug scooped up his Stetson off a nail on the back porch. It wasn't a real back porch just a little place where my grandma kept bags of potatoes and onions. On the wood slats between the stretched screens hung hundreds of rattlesnake rattles swaying in the breeze like wind chimes making the most delicate of sounds. For every rattlesnake my grandma killed with her hoe, she would hang their rattles like a trophy. She was the bravest grandma in the world, too. Grandpa slapped his sweat-stained Stetson against his legs, smoothed back his full head of hair and plopped his hat on his head. My day of adventure had begun.

Walking into the cool barn with sunlight slicing through the weathered wood sidings he'd lift me up on the haystacks so I could watch him lead Lucky out of the barn. He would speak to the horses in a low powerful but kind voice. He never used a switch or whip, just spoke to them with respect. Leading them out to the paddock, going round and round, lightly holding first a rope around their neck, then after a few days, would introduce a harness and bit, working gently, but still letting them know he was in charge. Round and round the horse would go with my grandpa in the center, slowly at first, then subtly increasing their speed. I'd watch my grandpa's face and then the horse's eyes and ears; they were one with each other.

After my begging, he would finally lift me up on one of the horses' backs, but never giving up the reins to me. Looking out from her kitchen window I could see my grandma smile. I could hear the screen door slam as she walked out to the corral wiping her hands on her apron, joining Grandpa Sug. They would walk the horse and me around the ring. I was in heaven. Not for many years would he let me ride by myself. I first had to learn how to saddle, feed, curry, brush, and most importantly, respect the horse before I was ever allowed to ride by myself.

My grandpa could rope, cut cattle, castrate steers, roll his own cigarettes while riding his horse with a single hand, (he kept the papers in one breast pocket and the tobacco in a little pouch in the other; he'd pull out a paper, while still holding the reins, reach in and pull out the pouch, pull the string of the pouch with his mouth, shake out the tobacco on the paper, pull the string again to close the pouch, stick it back in his pocket, lick the paper, roll it between his fingers and pop it in his mouth, strike a match on his jeans and light his cigarette), cut off his skin cancer with his knife and dab it with sheep dip, and love my grandma passionately. He liked his steak well done, and my grandma would always make two cakes for us. One for my grandma and me, and one dry as a bone for my grandpa. Just the way he liked it. She loved to please us both.

Their last home was in High Pass, California, out in the middle of nowhere. It was near the California and Mexico border, down an old dusty dirt road, nestled in a grove of ancient oak trees. It was a simple wood frame house of two rooms and a little kitchen with a kind of back porch. The only decorations on the walls were a picture of an Indian on horseback on a hill called "The End of the Trail," and another picture of a lone wolf baying at the moon.

Grandpa Sug worked as border patrol on horseback by then, not to catch people crossing the border illegally, but to catch cattle crossing the border. It was his job to make sure no hoof and mouth disease got into the cattle on the California side. I remember one time when Grandpa Sug was late coming home and both my grandma and I were worried. After sundown Dunny, his horse, appeared with my grandpa slumped over his saddle without his Stetson and bleeding from his head. He kind of remembers being hit on the back of his head by maybe a two-by-four, and I guess passing out, but Dunny kept him on his back and brought him safely home. Did Grandpa Sug go to the doctors? No, oh no. Grandma cleaned him up and stitched up the back of his head with her needle (of course sterilized by a flame in the kitchen, peroxide and silk thread) She was a remarkable seamstress.

At night when all the chores were done Grandma, Grandpa Sug, and I would sit by the potbelly stove. Grandma would play her guitar and whistle, and Grandpa Sug, rocking in his chair, would roll his cigarette and asked me, "Come on honey, get out your fiddle and play me *Red River Valley*." I hated that my mother would make me bring my violin with me on vacations, but I knew my grandma and grandpa loved it, and besides Grandma would slip me a lemon drop from her apron pocket as a prize after I played.

I look back on all the things I've learned from these loving, wise, non-judgmental heroes in my life. They number in the thousands. How to build and stoke a fire (first with kindling and allowing enough air between the logs), pull off my grandpa's boots, (back turned to Grandpa, straddle one leg at a time and pull from the heel with his other foot pushing on my butt), bake pies, cakes, biscuits (all with canned Crisco, butter, fresh milk, cream, condensed milk, not touching the batter too much to keep the air in it), fry the chicken only in canned Crisco, sweep and clean properly and slowly, feed and care for the horses, (not too much barley or corn because it upsets their stomachs and causes a lot of problems), ride a horse bareback or western, drive a stick-shift pickup, make a toddy for my grandpa (two lumps of sugar, a finger of whiskey and fill it up with hot water), iron what needed ironing (don't press or stretch the material too vigorously), respecting others, and loving the life you're living. Oh, and there's never enough catsup for your baked beans, per Grandpa Sug.

STAR WARS

PERU—TELEVISION AND THE ROAD TO MODERNITY

BY ALAN SLOAN

I chose Peru as the country where I would do my Ph.D. thesis fieldwork. Now that we were in Lima our first task was to get settled; no mean accomplishment. To help run the San Isidro apartment we needed five in help including two *muchachas* (maids) to clean the house and mind the children. Usually recent arrivals to Lima from the Andes mountain region, the girls worked six and a half days a week, shared the bare, cement block, backyard apartment (that had no hot running water) and were paid twenty-eight dollars a month. Parenthetically the twenty-eight dollars a month salary paid by most foreigners was considerably higher than the wages paid by our Peruvian friends and we often had to listen to the Peruvians bitching that we were undermining their economy and spoiling the help. As awful as it seemed to us, serving in an urban home was a major road to modernity for many of the indigenous inhabitants of the Sierras.

Nothing illustrates the cultural gap between those living in the Andes mountains and the Peruvians living in modern Lima than the evening we left Mabel, our maid, to babysit the children while we went to the movies. In a few short months, we had watched Mabel adapt to city life and mores. In her late teens she was very responsible and a real go-getter and so we had no hesitation in leaving her alone with the children. When we left the kids were in bed and Mabel was in the living room watching TV. We were attending the Peruvian premiere of *The Sound of Music* and it was particularly enjoyable because it was the American version with Spanish subtitles. Without struggling to comprehend a Spanish language version we could relax and enjoy a real US film.

When we arrived home after the movie, we were met at the front door by a distraught and frightened Mabel. She hustled us into the living room and, with shaking finger, pointed to a large hole in the plate glass window. *"Senor, el Santo disparo y casi me mata."* (The Saint fired and almost killed me). Mabel had been watching the British TV show *The Saint*. Evidently, in that episode, the Saint had been involved in a chase through a fog-bound forest. The antagonists had been hiding behind the trees and shooting at one another and one of the bullets sailed past Mabel, or so she thought. No matter how we tried we had not been able to explain to her that the TV was just stories peopled by actors who were playing parts. She absolutely believed that her life was in danger. I mean, after all, there WAS a hole in the window! As it turned out someone had fired a bullet from the street through the plate glass and into the living room. We discovered the bullet down the hall under Julia's crib. We felt violated and unsafe.

I called the police, who arrived almost immediately to take our statements. I also alerted the US Embassy and the next day embassy representatives interviewed us. It was then that we learned that our next door neighbor, who we had believed was a US businessman, was, in fact, an embassy employee. We suspected he was CIA and our imaginations began to get the better of us. We speculated that the bullet had been meant for our mysterious neighbor—we were living in the wrong place. Perhaps we should think about relocating.

Several days later we had another visit from embassy personnel. It was their judgment, and that of the police, that the incident was the work of the *roca y rodillos* (rock and rollers). These were gangs of young thugs who drove through the streets firing their pistols at well-lit windows. Their advice was that we were not in danger but suggested that if we continued to watch TV in the front room we should be sure to keep the lights off to avoid presenting a target to these delinquents. We replaced the window and from that time forward watched the TV in one of the back sitting rooms.

It took several months but we were finally able to convince Mabel that what she was viewing on TV was not real. She had watched Gene

Barry in the title role of the TV series *Bat Masterson* and had been fascinated by Barry's exploits in the American wild west. Soon after that program went off the air a new series, *Burke's Law*, starring Gene Barry in modern dress, premiered on Peruvian television. Mabel could not understand how Bat Masterson, cowboy gunslinger had become a dapper Beverly Hills police chief riding in a Rolls Royce limousine instead of on his trusted horse. Sally patiently explained to Mabel that most of what she viewed on television was not real and finally Mabel understood. She was beginning to grasp what modernity was all about. Mabel was extraordinarily bright and shortly after we returned to the States, we learned that she was no longer in service. She had married a Lima-based governmental employee and had become a full-fledged middle-class Limenan.

THE ACTUAL PRACTICE

BY LISABETH HUSH

The actual practice of being an actress
Requires more than a bed and a phone,
Usually it's tissue that's the additional issue
"Please cry us a real tear here, then give us a moan
Then weep us a spoonful as you gaze at the moon
Full of gloom for the lad in the tomb."

The art of illusion requires separate delusion
Depending on which sex you are nabbed—
The actress gives it the personal blush;
The actor, ten slaps for a nickel!
Even a woman of mystery is tied to past history
And usually heads for the door—no wonder their eyes
Are so sore—with peeping thru weeping and
Mascara all leaking, with bust pads that reach to the floor.

The invisible boundary is mistakenly found to be
Manned by males all hung-up on scores;
A misplaced appetite for sex really neglects the
Inequality purring out of celluloid pores.
Having to cry and not being asked why, are
Unequal requirements to the fair sex.
If the guys did the crying, shows would
Probably be more complex, and the appearance of a lady would
Maybe, just maybe, cause more than a craving for flesh/

Some women are happy
Being thought of as sappy
But some are making a fuss—

An actress's duty is not just her beauty
But to grapple with the very rough stuff.
Such as union poisons and all other kinds of rust.

WE'LL BE A DANCER

BY KAY WEISSMAN

Gertrude Doris Shubow was being groomed to be a great classical pianist, but when she debuted in 1931, she got a scathing review that damaged her life forever. She was unable to continue! She was only nineteen years old and her dream of becoming a great artist was over. One review became the tragedy of her life. And so she became a piano teacher and married Emil Friedman, a handsome Hungarian. They had a daughter. Her name was Wilma Kay Friedman. That was me.

I was seven years old, sitting at a baby grand piano with tears running down my little red face, playing scales over and over again until I couldn't bear it anymore. I screamed at my mother and said, "Just because you were a piano player doesn't mean I have to be one, please don't make me!"

"I would never make you do what you don't want to, but sweetheart, then what do you want to be?"

I was seven years old. I just wanted to be eight! I knew how much my mother loved her younger sister, the rebel, who ran away from home when she was fifteen to join a Russian gypsy dance company, so I said, "Oh Mommy, I want to be a dancer! My mother's face lit up. "Well, then that's what we'll be . . . we'll be a dancer!"

So after endless research, my mother found the perfect studio in Hollywood where I would begin my dance career first with ballet lessons and then I would segue into other styles. We had no car so we had to take two buses to get to Perry's Theatrical Studio on Highland Boulevard a world far away from Burbank where we lived. I was now eight years old and completely unprepared for what my first ballet lesson with Serge Oukriinsky would be. He was the teacher who would guide me to become a fine dancer. He was a Russian, famous for having once danced with the great Anna Pavlova. He was the real deal, but now years later his fame diminished. His classes were smaller so beginners and intermediates were put into one class.

When we got on the bus in Burbank, I had my new little dance case with the picture of a ballerina on the side, and inside was a tiny pink (my favorite color at the time) leotard, white tights, and pink ballet shoes. My hair was braided in two long blonde pigtails with pink ribbons at the end and my glasses were also pink. My face was pink too! I was prepared.

Perry's Theatrical Studio was not at all what I had expected even though I didn't know what to expect. It was an old building even at that time and, as you opened the front door, Mrs. Perry was sitting right there at her desk with a cigarette in one hand and the telephone in the other! My class was up the creaky stairs to the second floor where there were about four or five studios, each with different piano sounds coming from them. My heart started to beat faster in anticipation! There were other little girls in the hallway chattering away with their mothers already in their leotards. Most of them had on black leotards with their hair tied up in a bun. I was guided to the girls' dressing room that was filled with shelves full of all kinds of mostly smelly dance shoes. There was a cracked mirror also in the tiny room, and everyone was looking at themselves, admiring or criticizing what they saw.

We went into a small studio. I met Mr. Oukriinsky, a man of about sixty years with a bandage around his head. His face was covered with wrinkles maybe from too many years of disappointments. He was straight and tall and carried a stick which terrified me. He pointed to a place at the barre for me to stand and the music began! Not knowing the steps, I tried to copy what I saw the other little girls doing. Mr. Oukriinsky would call out names of steps in French, "*Plié, relevé*," and everyone seemed to know what he meant. The exercises were very hard to do and everything seemed to hurt me, but I did my best to keep up. He would walk around the floor with his stick, correcting small feet and arms and when he looked down at me, he smiled and had a twinkle in his eye. There was a little red-headed girl standing at the barre in front of me. She was beautiful with creamy alabaster skin. She must have been nine or ten and probably the best of all the dancers. I watched her and tried to copy what she did in front of me but it didn't look the same. I tried to smile at her but she didn't smile back. By now I was sweating and my face was red. I was not having a good time.

Somehow I got through the barre work but now it was time to do turns across the floor one by one. It was very scary because everyone would be looking at you. I went to the end of the line and hoped that something would save me from having to do those turns but finally it was time for me. I didn't know what I was doing and each time I tried to turn my pigtails flew around and hit me in the face. Finally after several tries my glasses fell off my face and I fell down. The redhead started to point and laugh at me. Then the other girls chimed in as well and everyone was laughing. I was humiliated. It felt like an arrow pierced my heart as I ran out of the room. My little eight-year-old brain realized that this was a very grave situation for me. I wasn't going to be a piano player, and now this meant I wouldn't become a dancer either! What would I be? What would I tell my mother? She looked stricken but stayed in her seat unable to move! I ran out of the room to the stinky girls' dressing room with tears falling down my face. I huddled in a corner hardly able to breathe when suddenly I was being cradled in the arms of Mr. Oukriinsky who unexpectedly was almost crying himself. "Oh Vilmitchka," he said, " I knew it the minute I met you, you have the soul of an artist, you are a special little girl!" I was eight years old and didn't know what a soul was or even what an artist was, but I knew that it was a good thing and that I was being protected in his arms. He smiled down at me, and at that moment I knew I had to continue dancing because I had the soul of an artist!

After a few years, I realized that I might have the soul of an artist but I didn't have the body of a ballerina. I did all the steps but it was never really good enough and although I loved going to Mr. Oukriinsky's class I hated the bus drive back. My mother would sit next to me and talk about the experience of the class and my performance. There was always criticism and comparison and even suggestions of how the steps should have been done, perhaps more like the little red-headed girl making me hate her even more than before. I never seemed to measure up to my mother's standards of how a ten-year-old ballet student should be doing. And then again, was it even worth all the sacrifice they were making spending money for lessons that I didn't take seriously enough? I thought I took it very seriously and cried myself to sleep every night wishing I was better at it.

After each class, I was flushed and sweating. I had to cool off with an alcohol rub and then sit for about ten minutes before I changed clothes. During that time I would run around and peek into the other studio windows that were covered by a thin curtain. Sometimes I would watch the contortionists and acrobats, sometimes a tap class with the great teacher, Ted Howard, where you could see famous Hollywood film stars tapping their brains out. The great Carmelita Maraci, would be teaching her exotic interpretation of ballet alongside Viola Spolen, famous for showing actors how to improvise using dance to express emotions. It was so exciting to see these great artists working. I was very lucky to take these wonderful classes, but minus the acrobatic contortions!

But one evening changed my life forever. I was sitting, as usual, drying off, getting ready to change clothes for the long bus ride home when I heard exotic sounds coming from the "big" studio downstairs. There were guitars and singing, stomping sounds different than the sounds of tap dancing. I ran downstairs and sat on the floor peeking through the frayed curtains. What I saw was electrifying! Exotic dark complected people clapping their hands to complicated rhythms.

Some were sitting in a circle singing and clapping, and others were dancing in front of them, shouting out to each other in a foreign language. I had gone to see the Ice Capades once with my parents, and I liked that a lot, but this was like a bolt of lightning, and something that made my heart beat faster. They were all so beautiful, not like anything I had ever seen before.

There was a lady in charge of them who was the most magical person I had ever seen. She had a red bandanna covering her black shiny hair, a long skirt, and big hoop earrings. She played something with her fingers that made a clicking haunting sound that seemed to rip into the music. I found out that her name was Lola Montes and she was rehearsing for a dance tour throughout California. Mrs. Perry whispered to me that she was a great artist.

On the way home on the bus, I was very excited and told my mother about the dancers. I was almost crying with excitement and begged her to let me learn how to do what I had seen. All week long I couldn't think of anything else.

Then once again we took the endless bus ride to Perry's Theatrical Studio. I looked up at Lola with glazed admiration. She told me she would give me a few private lessons before she went on tour, but not to expect too much. Little did she know about the gypsy blood that ran through my Jewish veins! *Viva Espana!*

And little did I know that something in my guts or my genes made it easy for me to learn the intricate dance steps that seemed to come so naturally to me. I just loved the fiery classical Spanish music of De Falla, Albanez, and Granados. Soon I was taking class with the adults and then, when I was twelve years old, Lola asked me to teach the class when she was away on tour. By that time everyone had a hand in changing my name from Wilma Kay Friedman to Antonia Flores and, with some help, my long hair slowly turned into a dark brown. At fifteen I went on tour with Lola in her company and learned to put on stage makeup including false eyelashes. I barely remember going to school as dance took over my life. I had to quit ice skating and horseback riding because they developed different muscles. Every penny we had went to lessons, costumes and going to see dance concerts.

There was one Spanish dance company that had become very popular in the United States. It was the Jose Greco Dance Company. He was very charismatic and handsome and his dancers were wonderful including gypsies, singers, dancers, and musicians. Everyone knew who he was and he became the darling of the dance world including Hollywood. When he came to Los Angeles to the Wilshire Ebell Theater, I got to sit in the first row no matter how much the tickets cost and I went more than once during the run. There was now no question that by age fifteen this was serious business for the whole family. My mother and father came to all my lessons and then rehearsals as well, both correcting me if I wasn't up to par. I rarely slept through the night, practicing steps in my head until I dozed off.

I idealized Lola as she had become my mentor. We found out that she also was Jewish but hid it from everyone. She warned me never to let anyone know that I was not Spanish. She always said that I reminded her of herself when she was my age and that made her treat me in a very special way that I adored. One day when I was twelve and had braces on my teeth, she took me aside during a lesson and pointed to another student. She said, "You see her? She isn't as good a dancer as you are but she is beautiful. You aren't beautiful so you have to be the best!!! Whish . . . it was as if an arrow shot into my heart! Not beautiful? My mother and father always made me feel that I was, and now I knew they had lied to me, so at twelve years old I knew I had to work harder than ever. My heart was broken, but I knew I had to be the best!

The year I graduated Fairfax High School with no memory of ever having learned anything was the year that the big news was announced. For the first time, the famous Jose Greco Dance Company was looking for only one dancer from the United States to join the company. This news spread like wildfire in the dance community. I was as ready as I ever could be and out of my mind with excitement. I knew it wasn't wise to tell anyone about the audition, especially Lola, so I prepared rehearsing with my mother playing the piano for me.

But now I was on my own without Mommy or Daddy at my side. I went to the Wilshire Ebell Theater where I had seen Greco dance so many times before, my suitcase with rehearsal clothes, castanets and dance shoes in my hand, ready to become Antonita Flores. This took makeup, a costume, and big Gypsy earrings. I could see the stage from the wings, the very stage that Jose Greco danced on and I couldn't wait to step on it. I wasn't afraid, I had prepared for this my whole life and I was ready! When my turn came I handed my music to Roger Machado, a great pianist who played for Jose's concerts. I couldn't believe he was actually playing for me. My music sounded like an orchestra. I did a dance with castanets and then a man's voice from the back of the auditorium said, "Do another one?"

When I finished he got up from the darkened auditorium and stood in front of the stage. It was Jose Greco himself. I felt faint. He asked me my name and I said it was Antonita Flores, which seemed to amuse him. He kept questioning me about my name over and over again getting the same answer each time. He then laughed and said "Okay, Antonita, we'll leave it at that if you insist. I want to talk to you!"

OMG. I think I stopped breathing. "He must want to tell me that he liked me, he wouldn't ask me to stay if he didn't like me!" So I waited for several hours backstage watching the other dancers. When they were done, Mr. Greco sat down with me and told me that I was the one dancer he wanted for his company when the season began; the only one who could fill the bill. He said he was going to make me a star! I was overwhelmed, and gushed and stammered, telling him how honored I was. He said his office would call me before the tour started. He hugged and kissed me. I believed every word he said . . . that was a mistake!

LETTERS FROM NEW YORK

BY ANNE FAULKNER

I n 1980 I resigned an executive position with Metromedia's television division, cashed in a number of stock options, and kissed Cincinnati goodbye. For some time I had been feeling that something was missing for me in Ohio. Work was great. The TV station ran smoothly. The Community Theatre's new season was about to start again. But, deep down, the nagging continued. Both my kids, Butch and De, were no longer living nearby, and I found myself becoming a people watcher. Wherever I was; having lunch, waiting for a bus, having drinks after work, I watched. And I wondered how many of those folks were happy in their jobs . . . in their lives.

At some point, I began asking myself the same questions, and my answers were clear. "I don't want to do this anymore," I thought. "I don't want to leave this world regretting not having done what I wanted to do most in my life. And acting is my life." My answers didn't surprise me as much as they scared me a little. But only a little.

My friends, associates, and fellow actors understood, and were one hundred percent supportive. It seemed as if everything happened rather quickly. I gave notice to Metromedia—a month, I think. My dad took over selling my house for me and I left him half my stock options for all he had done for me and the kids years ago.

With one suitcase and my old manual typewriter, I boarded the train in Cincinnati for New York City. I had never been to New York City. I had never been on a train. I had never risked much in life before, but now here I was risking everything. I was on my own, and I was fifty years old.

I wrote letters home, monthly at first, then less frequently as time passed, sharing my learning experiences with friends and family. Over *the years I had completely forgotten about those letters. Then recently, I received a package from my nephew. My brother had passed away, and his son thought I might want a box of things my brother had kept. I opened the box, and among old photos and memorabilia were my letters from New York. A lifetime ago. A pursuit of my dreams.*

I read them now, so grateful for the chance to take that journey again, and to remind myself that we are never too old to follow our hearts.

October 2, 1980

Hello...it's me again,
    In reading over my first letter,
I realized that I've said little...
or nothing substantial anyway, about
my impressions of the big city, or
any experiences other than those
theatrical. So I thought that this
time, I'd cover some of those things!
This city certainly isn't dull!! Okay,
first it's really easy to get around
here. Now, that's saying something for
me. As some of you know, I'm the worlds
worst when it comes to directions!
Almost all streets are straight and go
East and West, while all Avenues are
also straight but go North and South!
Basically every street (or avenue) is
one way, and there are buses that run
up or down each avenue, and across
every 4 or 5 streets. That may sound
very simplistic, but it really is! As
of now, I can run all over Manhattan...
easily, on the bus for $.60, and I'm
proud to say the walking has cost me 10

pounds!!! (which I have been happy to spend)

The people and human situations that you encounter here are mind boggling at first, at least compared to Cincinnati, but it's really funny how quickly you become nonchalant to most of those things. The first thing that impressed me when I got here was the box ladies, bag ladies, men, whatever. There are old ladies—and men, who have all their worldly goods in one or two shopping bags. They sleep in doorways, benches in the parks, and spend the day walking around New York, rummaging in the waste cans for food and drink that has been discarded by the rest of the hurried and rushed society that lives here... or visits here. Someone walking on the street flips a cigarette away, someone is right there to pick it up and enjoy one or two more puffs before it dies away. I was particularly impressed...on Central Park West, near 63rd street...a park bench that I passed daily while I stayed with Muriel. On it was the same old black man each day, seemingly sleeping, regardless of when I passed. Whether the temperature was 70 or 100, there he was, dressed in a heavy topcoat, and a cap with earmuffs pulled low on his face. He was very thin, and each day I passed I thought..." he isn't breathing"..yet I couldn't

stop to see. Something kept me moving.
I guess I was becoming a New Yorker!
I took Mom and Dad by there when they
were here...partly because I was
curious too, and sure enough, he was
still there.

My first venture into Central Park
was with Mom and Dad also. We didn't
go far, maybe 200 yards...but believe
it or not, far enough that we saw a
buy go down. (TV has taught me that
language) I couldn't believe it!! A
young business type white man carrying
a briefcase was walking along...
approximately half a block ahead of us.
He left the path and sat on a bench
next to a black man. He opened his
briefcase, so the lid blocked our view,
and the black man had a plastic bag,
half full of little packets.

Of course I couldn't stop and stare.
Dad made some wise comment jokingly to
mom and me about a 'citizen's arrest',
or going back in to see what was going
on (or some equally dangerous comment.
I don't remember exactly, but it scared
both mom and I to death, and we kept
him moving!!

The crowded conditions, cars, people
that you hear about are all true. Seven
days a week most of the city is like
Riverfront Stadium and the Coliseum all
letting out at the same time. There
are bike lanes provided on the streets

and a lot of bikers and roller skaters
getting from here to there. They ride
with whistles in their mouths, to blow
at cross streets, or to warn cabs and
buses that they are on the inside of
them...to the curb side. A lot are
hit I'm sure...because I've seen 4 or
5. I've not seen them actually hit,
but after they were hit...and while
they were waiting for the ambulance
or while they were being splinted,
prior to lifting and transferring to
hospitals. All young...both girls
and boys. That...I'll never get used
to. Accidents of any kind bother me
tremendously. The screeching of brakes
makes my heart skip a beat...(and that
you hear all the time in New York) I
wonder how often the cars and cabs here
must need new brakes.

I am a people watcher, and if I
tried to describe all the different
characters...I could write my book
now...after just these 2 months!!
Gals with lavender hair...or any
color to match their clothing. Men
or Women walking along, talking to
their imaginary animals (or maybe its
children!) Young men and women sitting
right out in public (Washington Square
Park) rolling joints...smoking...
passing back and forth, just like you
see on TV!! I know that if I'd ask for
a drag...they'd give it! Panhandlers...

men and men...women and women...the
entertainers on the streets, in the
parks...violinists, comics, singers,
magicians...the sharks on the streets
with their cardboard boxes and 3
playing cards, trying to suck in people
with the old carnie pod game. I really
hate to admit that I was sucked in...
but I will! I stopped one day, just to
'watch'. The guy flipped these 3 cards,
each under one of his boxes.. over,
under, across. There were 2 black cards
and 1 red one. All you had to do was
pick the red card! Of course I just
watched. Then one time, this guy picked
a card that I knew was wrong...I knew
where the red card was! Of course he
lost...but the guy didn't pick them up
and start over...he kept saying "pick
the red card". Well, I couldn't get to
my wallet fast enough to get out my
$20.00 and win a sure thing! Plus, it
wasn't a one out of three chance...it
was 50-50 and I knew where it was...I
had seen it!!! Well...naturally it
wasn't there...and I was probably set
up from the beginning. Maybe not...
maybe we were both sucked in...anyhow,
it was a $20 lesson that I won't have
to learn again...honest dad!) PS...
it was while you were both here, the
day I went out to pick up the "Annie"
tickets.
  I was on the bus going uptown one

day, and at Greely Square I heard someone on the bus comment, so I looked out, and low and behold there was a guy who looked just like Rosie Greer... (built like him anyway) standing on the corner...stark naked!!! (and I mean STARK) I couldn't believe my eyes! He was standing next to a police car and some old geezer was trying to get him to put on his pants. Three or four white police officers were standing around him and around them were a couple dozen other blacks. The guy was having no part of putting on his pants! The police weren't doing anything but watching! I must assume they didn't want to start anything if they didn't have to...because of possible repercussions. I don't know what happened, because the light changed and the damn bus moved on!!

My ULTIMATE 'people' experience however, happened yesterday. I was going to my TV acting class. I was supposed to be there at 9:00 am. I took the bus up 8th Avenue and got off at 45th. (Weist-Barron is on 45th) It was early...just 8:30, so I thought I'd stop for a cup of coffee at the Pancake house on that corner. I sat at the counter. A small black gal, Jamaican I think, was behind the counter. Near the door, and facing the front window was the grill, so a <u>large</u> black lady was

acting as cook and as cashier. Another
waitress, a tall thin black lady was
taking care of the tables in the
rear of the place. After listening to
conversation, I surmised the tall one
was the senior employee. My gal served
me...very slowly and disinterestedly.
I observed the cook was even slower!
In fact, I marveled at the eggs on the
grill which simmered there a good 15
minutes, while she played cashier...
very slowly. If you've ever seen those
rubber sunny side up eggs...I know they
not only looked, but I'm sure handled
better than these would when they were
finally served. At any rate, my gal
says to the cook..."where's my two
BLT's?" "You only ordered one" says the
cook. "I ordered TWO BLT's a long time
ago...these people have been waiting a
long time". Well...that started it...
back and forth they went. (In a way,
to begin with, the Jamaican had a
point...I never even saw the one the
cook acknowledged! Foul language soon
followed from the cook. The Jamaican
kept saying "If you don't want to take
my orders, I'll just tell the people
to leave" The cook would cuss again
and the Jamaican would say "The devil
is busy today". The cook was obviously
getting madder and the gal just egged
her on. Finally the tall waitress came
up and in an equally loud voice to the

Jamaican said ..."SHUT UP...you've made
your point, so shut up". And then to
both, as they each spoke, she'd say,
"Shut up". Both ignored her of course.
I felt that it was time for me to step
in, so I said..."check please". I may
as well not have spoken. The Jamaican
said to the tall one..."Don't tell
me to shut up!" and of course she
continued her tirade, adding that no
one could tell her what to do. A guy
who was at the other end of the counter
walked up to the grill and picked up
a plate with 2 pieces of toast on it,
saying..."Is this my toast?"...and then
carried it back to his seat. Of course
that just fanned the fire. The tall
one said to the Jamaican..."Customers
are having to wait on themselves...
now if you don't shut up I'm going to
smack you". Well...in short order they
were nose to nose with the Jamaican
daring the other to hit her. At that
point I thought maybe if I moved to
the register, I could get my check!!
Somewhere in the moment that followed,
a slap ensued and then they were on
one another...it was all out war! The
cook moved over...(faster than she'd
moved up to that point) to try and
separate them. The Jamaican bit!!
Threats passed back and forth. They
separated and the Jamaican picked
up the pots of hot coffee and water.

At that point I felt I was a little closer to the whole affair than I cared to be, however I was afraid that if I tried to leave without paying they'd all suddenly stop what they were doing and take it out on me. So I smiled, and took out my wallet. (they ignored me) "You throw that on me and I'll cut you" the tall one said. Now the cook was trying to calm everyone down. "I'm gonna call the boss" she said. "Give her a knife" screamed the Jamaican still holding the hot coffeepot. The cook dialed a number at the phone next to the register, and while she was waiting for an answer she looked at me and as calmly as you please she said "let me take your money". HONEST TO GOD!! Well, while she was making change for me, the boss answered and she told him that he'd better get over there. Now...I know that you are going to be disappointed, but at that point I left! Somehow I doubt that they killed one another. Sometime I'll stop in again for coffee...and see who's still there! Would you say that I've already turned into a blasé New Yorker??

Well...this letter has been on some of the oddities of human life, as I've seen it so far...in New York from Aug 10 thru Oct 1. More in the life and times of me...later.

    P.S. Ada seems no longer concerned
about my visitors or my entertaining
habits. What the hell does that
mean????

Love Sis

July 9, 1982

Hello,
 Needed to add this postscript...
Jury duty...never again! And, never
would I want to be judged by a jury. I
don't know if I can put into words my
feelings.
 "A person must be presumed innocent
until proven guilty, beyond a
reasonable doubt"...and "Deliberation
about that must not take place until in
the jury room at the end of the trial,
and after instructions have been given
by a judge"
 I was on 3 cases in 2 weeks...and
on all three, immediately upon locking
the door of the jury room, they all
wanted to vote! (their minds were made
up) On the first case, I was unfamiliar
with the process and I guess I hadn't
listened carefully enough to the judge.
I felt he was guilty, but had doubts
that robbery in the 2nd was the correct
charge. For plain robbery or larceny-
yes. At any rate I did feel he did it,
so I voted guilty. One juror abstained
because he had a question about the
victim being a participant in the
crime. We discussed, but regardless,
came back with a verdict in 15 minutes.
The judge made an off-hand remark about
the shortness of deliberation. That
really bothered me...

But then on the second case, I was
the foreman, so when they said "let's
vote," I forced a discussion for each
count. We took over 2 ½ hours and asked
for various information fed back to us.
The judge commented we had obviously
carefully considered the evidence!
We took long, but would probably
have reached the same decision in 15
minutes...had I not kept trying to play
devil's advocate! But at least I felt a
little better about the whole thing...
for MY part anyway.

After the second case and my
selection to be part of the 3rd jury
(when I penned the other letter) I was
already concerned about people, like
me... JURORS...coming to jury duty
because we are forced to, sitting in
judgment for case after case and most
taking it too lightly! Well, Case #3
did me in...but good! I wish to God I
had not been a participant!

A white girl, coming home at 4:30
AM was accosted in the lobby of her
building and robbed. The perpetrator
then took her to the roof, made her
disrobe, then raped and sodomized her,
beat her around the neck and back with
a nail or some sharp object and when
she feigned unconsciousness...left.
She crawled down the fire escape to her
mother's apartment where she was taken
to the hospital...and was there for

a week. She described her assailant as Hispanic with bushy hair, long sideburns, goatee and moustache.

Three weeks later, she was coming home from same subway stop. (4 blocks from her house)..and the way she had come home that night. Friends had been taking turns meeting her at the Subway entrance and walking her home. This night, her friend wasn't waiting when she got off the subway, so in a bit of panic, she went into the candy store there, to call her friend. When she turned around, the defendant was sitting on a stool. She ran out & told her friend, who had since arrived, that the man who attacked her was inside.

All the young people in the area know each other, or of each other, so Michael Johnsons name came out. Police questioned him, and one month later...arrested him. Then one month after that, they put him in a line-up. They had to wait so long because he had a broken jaw and they waited till swelling was down. Judge wouldn't let defense tell the cause of the broken jaw, but I'll bet it was caused by Beth's friends.

Prosecution witnesses were the victim and the young man who met her outside the candy store. Only other evidence by them was the picture from the lineup where she identified him, and picture

of puncture wounds on her back. The
Defense witnesses were the defendant,
his mother and girlfriend. Defendant
and his mother swore he was home in bed
at 4:30am. Girlfriend said that he had
left her at 2:45 after a party, saying
he was going home. Mother knew the time
because he had forgotten his keys and
had to ring the bell downstairs.

He cut his hair and shaved (all
but moustache) prior to arrest. He
said he cut it off way before June!
No one substantiated this, and the
friend of the girls who met her at
candy store said he had goatee at
that time. The saddest part of all...
the girl was 18 at the time, the
boy 19. The Defense (probably Court
appointed) unfortunately really gave
bad summation. Only valid thing he
said was there were no fingerprints
found as evidence from the door at
the roof...why no hospital reports
were introduced and why such a long
time from identification by victim
till arrest. Prosecutor said no other
evidence was necessary but the victims
word, if we believed that spending 1
hour with him on roof would certainly
indelibly imprint the attackers face
on her memory. She never identified
anyone else, and that the guys mother
had an interest in the outcome and
so the truth of her testimony or the

girlfriends should be questioned. Then
we went into the jury room.

The foreman said "well, shall we
vote?" I said, "How can you vote if you
are supposed to bring a presumption of
innocence into this room...especially
with how serious this is." Some agreed.
If we presume he is innocent...the
prosecution presented only the victims
account and the lineup identification
of the guy. It was very painful for
her to testify, no question a horrible
experience. He probably did it, but
a couple of things bothered me. She
originally gave description of bushy
haired, bearded Hispanic. Defendant
is a light skinned black. In the
identifying lineup picture, four
very black men and the light skinned
defendant were shown to her. Why no
fingerprints found to substantiate her
identification of him? Police came
at 6:00 AM, knew it had happened on
the roof and they had to go thru TWO
doors to get to the roof. The fact
that he shaved didn't bother me. I
can understand someone panicking and
shaving it off... and could still be
innocent. Especially if you are 19 and
a street kid. (not proved, but feel
it's so... kids that age out till 3 or
4:30) Isn't there a possibility that
someone else, who looks very much like
the defendant did it? Beard, sideburns

certainly obscure looks to some degree, and finally, they all lived in the area, probably passed each other before, maybe even in the Candy Store at the same time. Would he logically do that knowing they would undoubtedly run into each other again?

The Jury thought he was probably drunk or high. Anyhow....when it all boiled down, no one really believed the mother. Felt she was lying to protect him. There were discrepancies...the Prosecutor's cross examination was good. I finally thought if everyone else believed he was guilty, maybe my doubts were not really doubts...After all, the girl honestly and without question, believed that Matthew was her attacker. What would not finding him guilty do to her?

Anyway, when the verdict (guilty on all 5 counts) was read, he was very visibly shocked... and that surprised everyone because he had appeared so cool, and then he cried. His mother and young brother (12ish) and another friend, or relative jumped up.... screaming at us..."racists"..."I hope you can sleep tonight". The mother went on. "I told him all he had to do was to tell the truth"..."and "I" didn't lie". Well, the judge threatened contempt, told officers to shut her and the others up...the defendant was prostrate at the defense table! We were thanked and excused by the Judge.

The guards led us out, kept us in a separate room for about 10 minutes, then escorted us out of the building, but told us it might be better to leave outside, in groups...we did.

I came home, unplugged the phone and got more and more depressed. I still am...and I feel so sorry for all of them. Based on the evidence presented, guilty was the logical conclusion... HOWEVER, "Mistaken Identity" is always a possibility...isn't it? I would feel more comfortable about it, if there had been ANY hard evidence.... circumstantial evidence ...really enough?

Anyway, I wonder if the outburst had any effect on the other jurors. When we were locked away those 10 plus minutes, not one word was spoken by anyone. I wonder if they feel they gave him every break... I wonder if they ever want to serve on another jury.

ODD JOBS

BY KAY WEISSMAN

In the late sixties and early seventies, I was taking classes from Uta Hagan and Herbert Berghoff in Greenwich Village, living at the Winslow Hotel on Madison Avenue and 53rd Street, a very desirable address. I talked the manager of the hotel into renting me a tiny room that was previously used for storage, and I paid him by the month. I had a bed, a table with a hot plate, an old guitar, and that was it. I kept a jar of spaghetti sauce outside the window so it wouldn't spoil and boiled pasta in a little pan on the hot plate with the sauce every night for months on end.

On the weekend, I performed in an improv group called "Off the Wall" at the Riviera Café on Bleeker Street. During the day I took classes and went for auditions. I worked all kinds of temp jobs on the East and West sides of Manhattan. I would usually work for a week, just long enough to memorize the name of the company, and long enough to break their Xerox machines. I never lasted more than a week.

Having saved enough money from these temp jobs I was able to buy a hat check concession at a high-end steak restaurant on Central Park South called Marsh's Steak Place. Paying for the concession meant that I alone would receive all the tips, and hopefully, a cold winter would pay for my investment plus a little more. It was a great restaurant and my little check room was located right behind the front door, so I was the first person to greet customers, an ideal situation. I also put Shakespeare and other plays around my tip plate so the customers would know I was intelligent. Every night when I got home I would throw all my tip money on the bed and count each penny. I loved seeing the coins and dollars covering the little single bed, and it reassured me that I was taking care of business until I got my big break!

The restaurant had regular customers who would sit at the bar with their coats hung over the bar stools and never gave me a tip. I tried to be nice to them but I soon began resenting the dollar tip they withheld from my little pouch where I kept my tips stashed. One snowy freezing night the bartender and I were the only employees to show up for work. It didn't matter much because there were no customers anyway when all of a sudden a large group of frozen tourists entered the restaurant. I took them to a table. Since none of the waitresses were there to serve them, Danny, the bartender, told me to leave my position as hat check girl and take their orders. At that time in my life, my greatest desire was to be liked and admired so I was more than willing to handle the job even though I had never been a waitress and had no idea of the names of drinks or the brands either.

As I approached each person smiling my face off, my eyes glazed as they ordered drinks I had never heard of as if they were speaking another language. It never occurred to me to get a piece of paper to write it down. After all, I was an actress and could memorize anything. One by one they gave me their orders and I charmed them all with my little jokes as they asked for Dewar's on the rocks, Dewar's straight up, dirty Martinis, straight up Vodka, and many more I have forgotten except maybe in a nightmare.

When I got to Danny at the bar, still smiling as if I had won the lottery he asked me what they had ordered.

I looked at him blankly and said, "I don't remember."

Danny was not unkind but insisted that I go back and ask them again. My face felt like it was on fire as I returned to once again hear the strange language of liquor that I had absolutely no idea about. Looking back it is hard to believe that I was so green, after all, wasn't I the girl who escaped Burbank becoming a Flamenco dancer when she was eighteen? Didn't I travel all over Europe alone, performing in strange countries without a worry? Who was this idiot I had become who couldn't get a drink order right? Once again I went back to their table and asked for their orders and one more time all I heard were rocks and rolls, and all kinds of olive things with lemons to put in glasses, or whatever. This time Danny was not smiling and demanded I at least try "for God's sake" to tell him what exactly they had ordered.

I blurted out, "THERE WERE SEVERAL DON'TS WANTED, WITH AND WITHOUT ROCKS IN THEM, SOME WERE NOT DON'T BUT DOES, AND SOME OF THEM WERE STRAIGHT AND DIRTY, BUT I THINK A FEW OF THEM WERE GAY!" I said all of this with tears in my eyes as Danny jumped over the bar and took care of the situation. Luckily I kept my hat check job and then graduated to telephone work inviting people to come to a dinner where they were solicited to buy swamp land in Florida, but that's another story!

LYNDON JOHNSON AND ME

BY ALAN SLOAN

My real interests as vice president of the Stations Division were News and Editorials. Each local station was independent, but I received and reviewed copies of their editorials daily. And I was truly depressed by their lack of substance. Combining that with the numerous complaints received from local viewers concerning station news broadcasts, I was able to convince Bob Wood, then president of the division, that we had to expose the news and editorial directors to material that would add substance to their efforts. My idea was to convene a conference in Washington D.C. where the station personnel would listen to lectures from leading experts and discuss with them the types of problems facing their local communities.

It was a two-day seminar. The first day was devoted to the problems of the "Cities" and among the speakers were Patrick Moynihan and James Q. Wilson—a nationally recognized guru on urban problems. That day went very smoothly. At lunch, each table had a guest of some Washington prominence and Senator Robert Kennedy was seated at the head table between Jack Schneider and myself. I had a very friendly conversation with the senator who seemed genuinely interested in my experiences in Peru and my M.I.T. background. Schneider, in contrast, appeared almost hostile. Certainly not his usual charming self. Later I learned that when Jack was general manager at WCBS-TV, he had experienced some "very unhappy dealings" with the Kennedys and was still nursing a grudge.

The second day was devoted to the Vietnam War. Bill Kaufmann, professor of defense studies at M.I.T., a mentor and friend when I was doing my Ph.D. studies there, was universally respected in the defense community both for his research and his work for several administrations as a consultant to the defense department on both nuclear strategy and defense budgeting. In fact, in 1986 an article in the journal *Foreign Affairs* referred to Kaufmann as "the man who may well be the most knowledgeable individual in this country on the defense budgets of the past quarter-century."

I asked Bill to put together a group of experts who would represent a variety of viewpoints on this heated and divisive issue. And Kaufmann delivered—among the panel members were Daniel Ellsberg, at the time a senior Rand Corporation analyst and later of Pentagon Papers fame. Also Adam Yarmolinski, regents professor of public policy at Maryland University and former aide to Defense Secretary Robert McNamara. The discussion was spirited and I believe exposed the station participants to many new dimensions of the Vietnam controversy.

But the highlight of the day was a post-seminar visit with the President of the United States, Lyndon Baines Johnson, arranged by Johnson's close friend Dr. Frank Stanton, president of CBS Inc. All the CBS seminar participants, plus CBS Washington News Bureau executives and several correspondents, including Dan Rather and Marvin Kalb, were bused to the White House for the meeting. As we were ushered into a magnificent conference room, I couldn't help but reflect on the past several days. The seminars had been a great success and now I was awaiting the President of the United States. It was truly exciting and I was thrilled—but my "high" proved very, very short lived.

Waiters circulated amongst our group with drinks and petite-fours and after fifteen or twenty minutes the President entered carrying his toddler grandson under his arm. He signaled us to take seats. Jack Schneider, the senior CBS executive, and I were seated side by side on a couch directly across from the President. The atmosphere was cordial and friendly—the President making small talk with us while bouncing his grandson on his knee. After about five minutes his daughter, Lynda Bird, as if on cue, entered, took the youngster from the doting President and left. Then the President, getting down to business, turned to the group and as I recall said, "Now tell me what are you all doing here in Washington?" Schneider, preening with the importance of his CBS position, replied something like, "Mr. President, I'm Jack Schneider, president of the CBS Broadcast Group, and today we're here holding a seminar for our station news executives and editorial writers with defense experts to discuss the "pros and cons" of the Vietnam War."

I couldn't believe what I had heard and in the next instant, the mood in the room changed dramatically. For the President of the United States, there were no "cons" to his Vietnam policy and, glaring at Schneider, President Johnson asked him, "Who were those experts?" Schneider, looking at the President grasped that he had blundered and, recovering quickly, turned, pointed to me and said, "Mr. President, Alan Sloan is in charge of the seminar."

So there I was sitting across from the President of the United States. That enormous head looking directly at me, leaning forward in his seat like a huge grizzly bear ready to pounce. On the one hand, I thought to myself, I don't want to cause trouble for the seminar experts, but, on the other, if the President wanted the names he had only to pick up the phone to find out.

"Mr. President," I began, "the conference participants included . . . " and before I had spoken three names Johnson cut me off. He focused, laser-like, directly on me and then began what seemed like a twenty-minute monologue on "our boys" fighting and dying in Vietnam to protect us and the "American way of life." Throughout his entire recitation, it seemed to me that I was the sole object of his attention. Transfixed, I was paralyzed, totally unable to move. Finally, when he was finished lecturing me, the President got up, wished us all a pleasant trip home, and left the room.

As we filed out, Schneider pulled me aside and said, "I'm sorry I did that to you Alan, but you know I had to protect CBS." I shook my head in agreement, but we both knew that that was nonsense. He had goofed by trying to play "Mr. CBS" and in order to protect himself, he had diverted all attention onto me. I have always believed that was the beginning of the end of my career at CBS. Schneider knew that he had made a major mistake turning a friendly gathering into a confrontation with the President of the United States. I was witness to his faux pas and he knew that I knew that he had screwed up. From that time forward, although Schneider never outwardly showed any sign, our relationship would never be the same and eventually, I would be made to suffer for witnessing and understanding his weakness.

PASTIES AND RIM-SHOTS

BY DAVID KRAMER

My earliest memory as a child was of pasties, G-strings, and rim-shots. I was a showbiz baby, raised backstage in New York City's burlesque theaters; my dad's wardrobe trunk was my toy chest; baggy pants comics and strippers were my babysitters.

Gus Schilling was the first star I ever saw in person. A chinless Top Banana—Burlesque comics were never attractive men, their homeliness made them funnier. He was slim and tall, with a large belly and bulbous nose—and he was married to one of the biggest stars in the business, stripper Betty Rowland, the Redheaded Ball of Fire. Gus was a legendary comedian in many of the theaters where my father worked as a straight man.

Schilling was a good guy who shared the dressing room with my dad, and he enjoyed teaching me poker. He eventually won all my Tinker Toy trucks before he gave them back in a ceremony in which I swore that I'd never again gamble. I never did, not even in my Vegas years.

My father's dream for my future life was for me to become a burlesque straight man as he had been. I came close. When I was old enough, I became an actor. I struggled unsuccessfully until he died. Then I quit.

Not to gamble was only one of the lessons learned backstage amid the first and second bananas, talking ladies, crossovers-in-one, and exactly how the girls did the grind and bump.

When Gus and my dad were onstage together, one of the ladies of the ensemble would take me into the girls' dressing room, feed me chocolates, and play War, using pasties as chips. I'd stick around until the ensemble came storming in for a quick change. The moment that sequined costumes, G-strings, and bras started flying, I'd split. I was too young to know the benefits of hanging out a little longer.

I wish I could say that I grew bolder as I grew older, but I didn't. Many years later I'd arranged a *Playboy* magazine cover and tongue-in-cheek photo layout for my friend and client Leslie Nielsen, spoofing some of the greatest movies of all time. In each case, Nielsen was to be appropriately made up and costumed. He was to be photographed in every shot with at least one gorgeous young woman who was naked as a jaybird.

The spoofs were each to be one full-page photo created by the magazine's master lensman, Mario Casilli. Among the films were *The Three Musketeers*, *Rear Window*, *Gone with the Wind*, and, on the cover, white dinner-jacketed suave Leslie was to be James Bond—surrounded by a bevy of beauties.

I went to the Playboy Studio in Santa Monica, California, on the day of the shoot, and was greeted by the magazine's picture editor, Marilyn Grabowski, who led me to the room where Leslie was being made up and costumed for *Rear Window*. I stayed while he was made up. I stayed while he was placed in the wheelchair, and pushed to the set. I was there when they put the telephoto lensed camera in his hands, and when the models entered the scene. When they began disrobing, I left.

Some guys never learn.

THE SILENT HALLWAY

BY ANTHONY LAWRENCE

The stars are not in the sky,
they are in the silent hallway;
Sam and Hal and Billie Dove,
Ruth and Ida and the Brothers Nicholas.

Elsa, Walter and Roddy M,
with his face more ape-like
than the King of Kong.
Cary's there and Eleanor too,

with Elvis singing silent
on the white wall;
There's the Screen Smart Set
between the window light,

a mix of Ronnie, Greg and Mary P.
There's Jack Oakie and Kate Hepburn,
Marlene and Grace K,
and the still and gone forever grace

of Fred and Ginger
frozen in the cool and stagnant air
of a hospital just as MIA.
And sad Charlie sits in black-and-white

right next to Elizabeth T
whose beauty and youth grew into
the angry dark eyes of Virginia Wolff,
now fixed on your own face.
And Sophia L also stares at you on the far end
and you once again remember
her lips in Sunflower or Yesterday,
Today and tomorrow.
I think she's the only one still alive.
No, the stars here are not in the sky,
they are in the silent hallway,
never again to move or talk

or dance on their own, in the darkness
of the dream palaces where we watched
them in wonder, trapped like exquisite
dragonflies in flickering light.

raging potpourri

BY LISABETH HUSH

if and when it matters
that I married the ogre in me
recall after the newhall wedding
fay spain joined the tinny party
and sat on the lap of the groom
while he sniggered sappily and
told her he'd been hitched half
an hour before to me who sat in my
satin hat perusing behind its black
veil on what to pack for Arizona
and three days with the tv company
away from my groom's garbage of
emotional sophistry
if it comes to pass that anyone
cares what happened to me
if and when it matters that I
married the ogre in me
recall I dreamed in violence
that night of mockery
untouched and undesired in
tangled anxiety
with a fever and a cough
a rabid raging potpourri
I couldn't understand
The plan designed for me

IT'S A WONDERFUL LIFE

WALKING THE WALK

BY WILLIAM BLINN

They can call it what they want, but as far as my experience takes me, they cannot call walking any serious kind of exercise. You don't gasp; you don't sweat or cry out with teeth gritted effort. Granted, it does provide some window where stillness can be found, and there is something to be said for that, even if it needs to be said in a velvet whisper.

It was easy to get into the habit of the daily afternoon walk. Eventually, I came to recognize the faces on the walk around the lake. The two elderly ladies sharing bits of gossip and a lifetime of knowledge. The waddling fat man who thought a fifteen-minute stroll would erase a lifetime of indolent Happy Hours. The grimly determined UCLA coed who eagerly shared her youthful flowering with those of us who owned only the memory. There would be smiles exchanged, murmured well-wishing between strangers. Small comfort there. Not quite friends walking around the lake, though friends who shared the lake experience for a time. And if we could not back the night away, perhaps we could at least massage the twilight.

Then the walking about the lake underwent a dark transition.

The day was egg-yolk yellow and warm. Looking out over the unlit waters demanded a hard squint, so it is entirely possible that I failed to register each of the regulars as they made their respective appearances. Mister Waddlebutt was there, and the gaggling gaggle of Gossip Girls was there, too. I could see Miss UCLA in the distance offering her bouncy breast best. All was right and in place until the tremor.

It was a tremor I had known before, almost for all my adult life. I had not experienced it for possibly forty years and it stopped me dead in my tracks, throwing me into that wide straddled stance normally associated with tremors we label on the Richter scale.

Cigarette smoke.

That's what it was. A puff of memory going back to the time when I was fifteen, maybe younger. Bear in mind I was not trolling in a Pittsburgh beer hall, mid-1940s. I was slow strolling around a Southern California lake, a state in which the word "green" denotes far more than a selection out of a Crayola box. I am of the generational mindset that places smoking next door to sexual predatory moves on a five-year-old.

I have been a smoker. Don't tell me it's hard to quit. Don't presume to say that because a thing is hard, it cannot be achieved.

Do I sound merciless? Very well. I sound merciless.

There was a large shrub at the next curve in the walk and a billow of cloudy gray poison told me the lung shredding sonofabitch was puffing away just around the bend. I didn't know what I was going to say to him, but there was no question that I would have some haiku harangue that would scald the scrotum of his soul in the most appalling way. I swung wide when I can to the final curve and edged out to one side in order to maximize the sightline to my advantage.

The hair was silver and the wardrobe indicated there was some wealth at hand. The soft breeze brought not only the toasty scent of death stick, but, in addition, the floral snare of an appealing cologne. I estimated the age to be in the seventies. And she was really quite attractive, were she not smoking. Then she leaned forward and bent low, reaching under the bench where she was seated so placidly puffing away, reaching down and behind herself to pet the dog lying there in the shade. Big dog, color of rich brown leather. Its body arched up toward her as she scratched its head. The dog was a pitbull.

Had I the mystical power to snap my fingers and remove all pitbulls from the face of the earth, that finger snap would take place more swiftly than sunlight and heat would mate. Collies do not rip three-year-olds to shreds. Labrador retrievers do not gnaw greedily at screaming old women before lapping at the results of their volcanic need to feed. These horrific attacks spring solely from pitbulls and if all are not guilty, then that is equivalent to asking understanding for those cancers that are not terminal. I say they are dangerous to the innocent and deserve no hearing. Finger snap—finger snap—finger snap.

Even as this reactive revulsion tightened my gut, I continued to close the distance between the smoker and her solemn-eyed beast. She stoked its sloped forehead fondly. Its fur was the color of sun-cracked saddle leather.

The smoker looked up as I paused before her. "Not supposed to do that," I said.

Her patrician brow furrowed. "Not supposed to do what?" she said.

"Smoke," I said. "There are kids around."

She looked up the walk one way, then the other. "I don't see any children," she said.

"Well, no, there aren't," I said, hating myself for starting this conversation. I was an old fart hectoring a complete stranger who had been minding her own damned business. Get off my lawn. Turn down that music. God, what an old fart. I leaned down slightly, seeking to make eye contact and allow some of the tension to leave the air.

As I bent forward, the pitbull made a sound. Not a growl or anything like that, but a pitbull sound nevertheless, and that's all it had to be to restore my unreasoning edginess. I glared down at the dog. "Is that a pitbull?" I said.

"It is."

"I don't see a leash."

"He doesn't need a leash."

"Dogs are supposed to be leashed in the park."

"Sir, you are the most unpleasant man I have ever had the misfortune to deal with." She started to gather her purse and its belongings, sitting up straight prior to getting up to leave. "There are security guards around here and I intend to tell the first one I see that you are harassing me. I will file a complaint and the police will be called and your family will have to deal with the sad business of confronting the fact that Grandpa has finally lost it and is now badgering old ladies in the park." The pitbull made another territorial declaration. She glanced down. "Maynard, hush."

"Maynard? You named your goddamned dog 'Maynard'?"

"I did."

"What kind of name is that for a dog?"

"When I call him, he comes. Seems to work."

I took a step back, both hands raised in a gesture of surrender and apology. "Look," I said. "I am not a total jerk, and I'm sorry we got off on the wrong foot. Smoke all you want and name the damned dog whatever you want."

"It was my husband's name," she said.

"And a damned fine name it is," I said. "I won't be bothering you anymore today." I turned my back and started off in the opposite direction.

"Then when?" I heard her call.

I stopped, looking back. "Excuse me?"

"If you aren't going to bother me anymore today, just when are you going to bother me? I'm here by ten o'clock pretty much every morning."

"Look, Mrs. Whatever your name is . . . "

"Kellogg," she said. "Mrs. Maynard Kellogg."

I didn't move. Nor did Mrs. Maynard Kellogg. She just looked back at me, bending in a half crouch, scratching the short fur on her dog's skull. Maynard the Devil Dog looked at me solemnly. Its stubby tail twitched.

"Mrs. Kellogg?"

"Yes . . . ?"

"Do you like Italian food?"

FRED

BY PHIL HABERMAN

There's a hummingbird in my backyard. His name is Fred. In the afternoon Fred and I sit back there and listen to music. Sometimes we sing together. Well, I sing, Fred chirps. Fred has a great voice. A great chirp? Whatever. Fred has perfect pitch. I sing off key a lot. He just looks at me. Shakes his head.

The first time I saw Fred was about a month ago. He flew into my backyard and landed on the back of a chair across the table from me. I was listening to Jack Teagarden singing "A Cottage for Sale." Fred started to sing with Jack. It was magic. Like they had been singing together for years. When they finished singing, I applauded. Fred spread his wings and took a bow.

That was the beginning. He visits every day now. I put food and drink out for him. Built a perch for him to rest on. We just sit there. Sing and laugh. I was listening to Willie Nelson one afternoon when Fred few into the yard. Willie was singing one of my favorites, "Night Life." "Night life, it ain't no good life, but it's my life." Kinda sad. Fred loved Willie. They sang together often.

Days passed. All of them filled with songs and laughter. July went by. August. End of summer. Fred would be coming by soon to say goodbye. He would be going south for the winter. The next day Fred flew into the yard. I held my hand out and he landed on my finger. I held him close to my face. His beak touched my lips. He chirped goodbye and flew off. Goodbye, Fred.

The leaves of autumn came and went. Christmas. New Years. The winter winds. Springtime. Would Fred be coming back? One day I was listening to Frank Sinatra. The song was High Hopes. I started to sing with Frank. "I got high hopes. I got high apple pie in the sky hopes." Fred flew into the yard and onto my shoulder. He was singing with me and Frank. I was singing off key. Fred looked at me and shook his head. Freddy's home. I shed a tear. "Dream. Sometimes dreams can come true."

One day not long ago, Fred flew into the yard with three of his friends. I was listening to the Four Lads singing "Standing on the corner, watching all the girls go by." Fred and his friends joined in. It was quite a show. Eight-part harmony. After Fred had been with me for three or four weeks, I think he began to understand, to recognize some words. I, in turn, thought I understood some of his chirps. One afternoon Fred began chirping more than he usually does. I thought, maybe . . . ? I put on a Rosemary Clooney CD, "Come ona myyy house, ahma gonna give you caaandy." There was no stopping Fred now. I became a disc jockey, and Freddy began making requests. Happy times. Fun times. Fred made each day The First of May.

In late June of that year, Fred met a cute little Hummer. They flew off to Catalina to start a family. I never saw him after that. He sends me a card now and then. It's not the same. Maybe, someday? Another hummingbird? Dream.

TWILIGHT

BY SHIRLEY COHEN

Twilight is that magical atmospheric miracle that occurs both morning and night. At dawn, before the sun rises, the sky brilliant with oranges and reds and, and sometimes with wondrous clouds, there are pinks and grays and blues all at once, too quickly fading, but promising a new day and a fresh start . . .

But my favorite twilight is before dusk as the sun slowly sinks below the horizon and the moon begins its rise to take its place among the stars with hues of lavender and pink and lilac and luminous shades of blue. And how wonderful to be near the ocean to watch the sun slip into the sea, the sky full of orange and red and pink and blue and gray when there are clouds, a thrilling spectacle for only a few moments to drink it all in.

I feel so fortunate to be allowed to be where nature abounds at this heady time . . . in a garden when night blooming flowers begin to open and broadcast fragrances delighting my senses. With time to inhale the quietude and wonder of night gently falling all around me, when nocturnal creatures animal and human begin to steal from their lairs preparing for adventures in the darkness.

THE CUTTING EDGE

BY DUKE ANDERSON

Even though the Navy owned me body and soul until the war ended, my father from miles away at home still did little things to make my life a little better. He had done that all my life.

I wasn't on board my ship very long when I got myself a buddy, practically from home. Marvin was from Hollywood, and even though I was from North Hollywood, he and I had many places, streets, people and things we were both familiar with. Our high school teams played against each other in sports once in a while. We both loved big band music and had frequented the Hollywood Palladium to hear the bands. We both shopped at the same stores in Hollywood. There weren't very many Californians on board my ship, so Marvin and I had that in common too. Even though Marvin was from Hollywood, his dad had a boring job in a boring place. Me, on the other hand; my father was in the exciting world of the movies. So, in a way, I was more genuine Hollywood than was Marvin. On board ship, I took great advantage of that.

I was in the K-Division which totaled about thirty officers and men. We were the radio gang. Radio and Communication Intelligence. They soon learned that my father was in the movie studios and wanted me to give them all the gossip. I was more than happy to do that. With an "aw shucks" sort of attitude, I would tell them whatever I could come up with. Some of my stories were true. Things I had heard my father say at dinner times through the years. I mean my father knew a lot of the movie people, so that was almost the same as if I knew them, wasn't it? And after all, I had spent many hours on the studio lots through the years. My shipmates didn't absolutely have to know that many of those hours were actually spent on the back lot playing in the western set, or in the mock airplanes, or whatever else was back there. Until a guard would discover we kids and kick us out.

My dad would go to the head still-photographer and get 8×10s of all the pretty starlets and send them to me. Many of the girls, not knowing me from Adam, but thinking they would be helping win the war in their own way, would autograph their pictures to me personally. You can't believe what that did to my reputation on board ship. So I became the Hedda Hopper of my ship. Some of the Officers in my gang wondered if they could visit me if we got a leave home. They asked me to join them in their Chess Club. I was the only enlisted man they asked. Ah, The Power of Hollywood. Oh, yes I would say, "The things that girl does behind closed doors." They were enthralled. Actually I had no idea what that girl or any other girl did behind closed doors. In fact I wasn't really sure what anyone did behind closed doors. I was still a teenage virgin. Some necking in the movies and in some of the darkened dens during house parties, but that was about it. My imagination spurred me to come up with some great tales, however. Well, they were practically true. I mean, pretty close. Fortunately for me and my tiring imagination, after a few months this Hedda Hopper stuff simmered way down.

Another thing my father did; he had a knife made for me to carry with me when I was on board ship. When he found out I would be on a ship out in the Pacific, and knowing most sailors carried a small knife he went to props and found a real German Bayonet they had used in some picture. He gave it to some guys on the lot who knew what to do. They made it shorter, discarded some of the fixtures that allowed it to be connected to a rifle, and someone else made a holster for it.

When he gave it to me, we shared our feelings about not ever wanting to kill. Anything. He wanted me to have the knife for my protection. He said, "You don't want to kill, I know. Hopefully you won't get into that situation. If you're shipwrecked and end up on an island, you can use this to dig out roots to eat. You can use this to strip saplings to make yourself a shelter. If you're in the water and you run into sharks, well . . . " He told me the decision to kill or not to kill would naturally be mine when the time came. Fortunately, I never had to make that decision. I'm not quite sure what I would have done. That knife, though, was always a comfort for me to wear. I carried it with me the rest of my time onboard ship. I still have it. It's not as sharp as it once was. But then neither am I.

MY JOURNEY TO THE DINING ROOM

BY DEBORAH ROGOSIN

Well, it's time for lunch and my guide dog, Asha, is tired from running at the dog park so I'm going to grab my white cane and walk the two blocks from my cottage. I must be careful since, after all, I did fall over a dolly that someone left in front after moving in some boxes. I badly sprained my ankle! I also want to familiarize myself with the last leg of the walk near my cottage, so I can tell Asha when to turn.

I grab the longest white cane, about five feet long, that gives me a good distance between my hand and the ground. I walk outside and drag it from side to side putting it on my right as I step with my left foot and on the left when I step with the right. It's very important to keep the edge of the walk on one side or the other so I can understand where I am. I know some people tell me to walk a little to the right or a little to the left so I stay in the middle of the path, but if I do that I can't tell when to turn and I miss the landmarks. I must remember that people's intentions are good, but sometimes their comments aren't helpful, like, "Watch out, there's a cart in front of you."

Both my white cane and Asha recognize that if something is in front of me, they both go around. Also when I have Asha with me, people don't know that they shouldn't talk to Asha, when I have the handle in my hand. It only distracts her.

The one thing I am concerned with is walking into a person.

I walk out the front door, keeping my cane on the left. I know there is a bit of a drop-off where I turn left so before the week is up I'll fill that in with a little planter mix. I turn left, counting my steps and keep the cane on my left, moving it back and forth but touching the left. When the sidewalk slopes down I know it's just a few more steps before my left turn when it becomes flat. I must remember to be careful on that curve. It's easy to lose your balance on a sharp downhill turn. That was about forty-five steps from the front walk. I now have a sense of it. In a short time, it will become second nature to me. I turn left and go down to Elm Street.

It's a beautiful day, the sun is warm but there's a cool breeze. The birds are singing in the trees and I hear a crow about a block away. It's about fifty-five steps to Elm.

I make a left jog at Elm, take a couple of steps and travel down the Hill, following on the left with my cane. I pass Pine and am very comfortable walking down that bumpy slope. My feet are so familiar with. There is a squirrel in the tree. Asha would be a little distracted but she's getting used to them. At first, I held on to the rail on my right but I've learned there's rose bushes there and I don't want to get scratched. Also, if I walk too close on the right there's a big drop-off.

I hear a ping with my cane, a piece of cement, and it reminds me I'm near the turn, about four steps on the left near the bottom of the slope as it levels off. As I arrive at the bottom where the pipe rail ends and turn into Ash Street, I go right and start to trail the right side and feel the intermittent short brick walls between planted areas. I always remember my trainer's words at Guide Dog School, "Pick up your feet!"

First I pass Joan's cottage. She never seems to be coming or going but I have left books from the book club at her door. There are often laundry or cleaning carts, but there is room to pass them. Then comes Maggie's, and I sometimes meet her on the path and we talk and laugh a bit. I pass a few more cottages as my feet feel a slight rise then a slight peak and then a slope down again, and I continue on as the path widens.

I think about the topiary there, especially the giraffe and have to smile. I feel the entrance on the right to the new Green Room, which is fun to visit sometimes and continue straight across an intersecting path. At the beginning of the next section, Lacy usually starts to bark so I know I'm coming to Carol's—Cottage #6. There is a short wall there, and I switch to trailing it on the left. At the end of the wall, I face eleven o'clock and walk nineteen steps to the bridge. I'm familiar with what's on each side of the bridge at the entrance so I know where I am if I've overshot it. Sometimes I do get distracted there saying "hello" to friends.

At the entrance of the bridge, I listen for footsteps and try not to cross when someone else is there. I'm also very careful not to touch the sides of the bridge with my arms or hands since I have gotten splinters. I hear the sound of the fountain and sure enough, there is a crow nearby, thirsty, noisy little guy. Sometimes I smell roses blooming here.

At the end of the bridge, I go straight toward the dining room entrance, feeling my cane hit the grass on my right. I trail it on the right with my cane for a few steps and then cross over to the entrance to the Country House. When I hit the grassy edge I keep the cane on my left and trail towards the door.

Often there are carts there or other distractions like people trying to help me, or talking to my dog, so I trail around them. (Perhaps I should write a paper showing how they can be helpful to a blind person since I'm sure most people would like to be helpful if needed.)

I've familiarized myself with the architecture in front and the landscaping at the entrance, so I'm not usually lost unless I'm daydreaming which does happen occasionally. I hear the automatic doors open and I go through the door.

I reach for the edge so I don't bump into it, I then swing around, while hearing the music to the right, and pause near Chuck's table, since there may be waitresses or residents chatting there. I begin to smell the delicious odors of what food is being served, and sometimes I can guess what it is. Usually, there are a few "hellos" there, so I concentrate going past the second table on my left table straight to mine. The table has four legs rather than one in the center, so there is room for my dog underneath. I check that out before I sit down.

The table is set nicely with cloth napkins. I check to see if the outside of the glass of water is clean, and I take a drink before the server comes to kid with me and take my order. Around me are the familiar voices of the residents chatting away. It gives me a feeling of familiarity and security.

Lastly, I hear Joel come in from his work at Channel 22, which is becoming a kind of second home, and he announces himself with a lengthy hug, a sometimes too-ardent kiss, or a questionably intimate touch, and as he sits beside me, I feel loved.

ONE GREAT LIBERTY

BY BRETT HADLEY

Sasebo Harbor is huge. A fine place to ride out a typhoon. A better place—though not safer—but far better, it was my good fortune to find: a haven of sensual joy for a twenty-one-year-old sailor, riding out a typhoon in a Japanese cat house.

Leaving a ship of steel for a house of paper and wood during a humongous storm is on the face of it stupid and a might short-sighted. But, that is also the definition of a young sailor with three months of no shore leave.

I was not a member of the *dress blue navy*, those men of battleships, carriers, and cruisers, admirals, and lots of gold braid. I was in the *dungaree navy*, the amphibians, LSTs (Large Slow Targets Navy). Being disposable, we were not given preferred berthing; that is, not dockside berthing or even close-in mooring. We were delegated to swing at anchor on the very outer edge of this immense harbor. A ninety-minute boat ride, ship to shore. Thirty randy kids standing for ninety minutes in the well deck of an LCVP (Landing Craft Vehicle Personal).

Our liberty orders had been written by our Captain (a grade school, reservist lieutenant called up for the Korean Police Action). Basically, being a civilian, he was not too savvy when it came to cre-ative interpretation, especially the interpretations of randy young *sea lawyers*. There was an "if" in the orders. "If the typhoon strikes and you miss the last liberty boat, take shelter and we will collect you when the storm passes." The magic "if" that opened wide the doors of possibilities. Of course, we would miss the last boat; it was missed the minute we left the gangway.

Within ten paces of our boat, Fritzee and Claude, the most horny of all men, had corralled three wenches of pure Asian beauty.

There is an old adage, "Beware the East. Once smitten, you are hers forever."

The winds and the rains were building fury. The six of us took emergency measures and stocked up enough sake, beer, and food for what we hoped would be three days of the adrenalin high of danger and sex.

Alas, it was not to be. The storm took a left turn for China and for the most part, passed us by. Not, however, before much sake and Asian love had been had. Then back to sea it was. But what a great liberty it had been.

FROM L. A. TO SHINING SEA

BY DAVID KRAMER

Being of the Hebraic persuasion, I was deemed a man upon a Saturday morning recital of *brouchas* and a reading of a section of the Torah specifically for this date.

I later learned there was more to being a man than *brouchas* and gold fountain pens. It had to do with learning to love a woman, or in this case, a girl from the Edenic isles of Hawaii.

Enter Maile Darlene Haulani, a Tahitian dancer, a blessing—and a curse. She was beautiful, smart, volatile and sensual. She was also crazy . . . and for some reason, she became the standard, the model of what I sought in women ever after.

My kind of crazy woman isn't given to running through the streets nude while screaming and foaming at the mouth. Not that crazy. Just impossible to tame. Or understand.

They were smart and funny, more a woman partner than a girlfriend, and as a lover, provocative, inventive, responsive . . . all fine qualities. However, it would be wise to keep the knife drawer locked, and gather everything that might act as a blunt instrument and bury it all in the backyard.

Actually, the way we met would have warned a normal man. So as I go along with this you might come to think that your narrator is also a few bricks short of a load. Here's the set-up. Come with me to yesteryear and picture a bar with a musical quintet on a small stage abutting a dance floor about twelve feet square. It's called The Penthouse, with a street-level elevator that went only to the second floor. Cute? In 1947 it was a hangout for my crowd, young men and women who danced the Lindy, or Lindy Hop. It's still around, now called swing dancing.

One weekend my pal Gil showed up with a bleeding gash on his forehead, and a wild-haired brunette visibly seething with anger. Gil tells me they'd met over the phone and made a date for tonight. Gil had brought a pint of Chivas that they chuffed along the way from Culver City to the Penthouse.

"So we're doing okay, and she's taking a hit off the bottle, and I felt like copping a little feel, and I did—and *wham*, bitch slams me with the bottle! Damned near went off the road . . . you'd have thought I did something wrong f' Chrissake."

By now, the girl's found a table in the dimmest part of the club. She's gotten a drink and was half hidden in the dim lighting. She'd sip the drink, puff on a Tareyton, and cast an evil look at Gil, then start all over again.

"I'm scared to death of her . . . can you take her home? She lives near you . . . come on, be a pal?"

I took her. It was a long drive, and along the way, I realized that she was spirited, smart, and fun to talk with. So, when I dropped her off and asked for a date, she gave me her number, and I promised to call.

It wasn't until I was almost home that I realized she had to be in her twenties . . . how do I tell her that I'm fifteen and just look older because of my heavy beard shadow?

We had a great time on our date, and were holding hands and kissing, when she pulled back, and said, "I have to admit something, and I'm scared that I might lose you . . . I'm only fifteen . . . "

Well, birds sang, BELLS RANG! It was terrific. We became a couple and had fun both vertically and horizontally. But it was a stormy relationship. Sometimes we'd make plans, and I'd show up at her home and she was nowhere to be found.

We'd fought one night on our way to a house party, and I didn't see her again until it was time to leave. I finally found her in a small room, necking with my friend Chuck.

Now that you know a little about us . . . is it any wonder that we were in and out of the relationship for seven years? Of course not.

It helped that when the war broke out in Korea, I volunteered for the Navy, and was seldom home on leave, but seeing her again . . . I was just as smitten as I'd been on our first date.

In March of 1955, I was discharged and drove up to her house, whereupon we'd planned to go somewhere and share a bottle of champagne, toasting to being together again.

I drove up the coast in my new (used) red Pontiac convertible. I arrived at her home. Her mother had no idea where she was. Gee, I was a little annoyed. On the way to my folks' home, I was screaming and pounding on the steering wheel. I never called, nor did she call me, but I'd see her name in the trades from time to time.

In 1957, I was studying acting with Estelle Harmon and looking for an agent by day, and driving a taxi by night. One night I pulled up at the stand across from the Beverly Wilshire, asked a driver to watch my cab and started to cross the parking lot to a phone booth to call my service in case I'd missed a call from Daryl Zanuck or Jack Warner. I heard my name called out, turned, and saw someone waving from a silver Corvette. I didn't know anyone with a Vette, so I kept walking, and then I heard the chatter of high heels on asphalt and turned to see Maile.

"Well, don't you have anything to say to me?"

"No, Maile, not a word," and I turned and walked away, never to see her again. In a way, I won but never was happy about it.

Never, ever.

Oh, when I finished writing this, I went online to see if I could find her, and after just a few clicks I did. Maile Darlene Haulani died in1976.

She was forty-four.

THE DINNER

BY KAY WEISSMAN

When I met Murray I was living in a small garage apartment behind the swimming pool of a complex in Burbank. I put two exotic plants in front of my door that faced the pool and fantasized that I was living in Tahiti. The rent was nominal and I was near the theater group I belonged to where I spent most of my free time. I was not suffering at all living like this, happy to be a working actress, paying my bills and taking care of myself. It was the way I lived for most of my life, kind of like a gypsy performer, living out of a suitcase at times and spending money carefully, always wondering when the next job would happen. It was just the way it was, nothing to be sad about, just a frugal lifestyle with very few luxuries.

Murray swept me off my feet for sure. I think he thought of himself as Richard Greer, and me as Julia Roberts in *Pretty Woman*, except for the prostitution part. He told me later in the marriage that he couldn't wait to rescue me from my difficult life and to give me things I never had had before. I never thought I needed rescuing, and since I fell in love with him so quickly I never questioned his motives which thankfully turned out were always just to bring me joy. Our romance could easily have been made into a movie, and from beginning to the end it was like a sudden burst of Technicolor. Our honeymoon began in New York at the daytime Emmy's where we walked down the red carpet! I couldn't believe we ate three times a day since I was always on a diet in my past life and always worried so much about my weight. I don't think I ever ate a cookie before I met Murray, and he got a kick out of my saying "this is the best meal I ever ate!" after each meal, and oh how I loved room service for breakfast. We segued to magical Paris and then Madrid, where I got to show him where I had lived and performed in my past. I proudly took him to the Rostro and showed him where the gypsies and my teacher, La Quica, lived. We wound up in Calpe, Spain, in a mountain retreat that reminded us of the old movie, "Lost Horizon" where Ronald Coleman discovered "Shangri La" because it was surrounded by puffs of clouds.

There were many other trips, cruises and exotic places that tickle my memory and bring a myriad of feelings back to me as I live day-to-day, but the one I want to talk about today was our favorite place in Italy, Positano, on the Amalfi Coast. If there really is reincarnation I would hope to somehow be placed there in my next life, perhaps as one of the magenta bougainvillea trees or maybe one of the delicious gigantic lemons used for a limoncello aperitif!

On our fifth anniversary, we went to Rome and then spent a week in Positano living in a magnificent hotel overlooking the Mediterranean Ocean. We went to a place for lunch called Le Sirenuse Hotel, famous for celebrities and European luxury and had a delightful meal. The roads are very steep there and no cars can go through the town of Positano because the streets are really just stairs, so we were grateful that we were both able to walk and enjoy this fantastical holiday that we never forgot and often talked about.

On our fifteenth Anniversary we once again went to Rome and wanted to go to Positano but that would have been impossible for Murray to handle the steps and maneuver as by then he was walking with two walking sticks or a cane. We decided to hire a driver and go from Rome to Positano and just drive up to the Hotel Sirenuse in time to have dinner and then drive back again, so that's what we did. We arrived in time to see the sun set on the Mediterranean Sea in a window seat at the restaurant, and, as it got darker the waiters all got very busy lighting candles. The whole restaurant was lit with about one hundred candles hanging like elaborate chandeliers, looking like diamonds or stars. All of a sudden several musicians appeared playing mandolins going from table to table, serenading us. The smell of the pasta was intoxicating and the wine was flowing. Because it was our anniversary they serenaded us endlessly, as we held hands and felt the exquisite joy of life and love. We knew it was a special moment in our lives and vowed to never forget it. We never did!

A SONNET TO RACHEL

BY SHELLEY BERMAN

My daughter, how can I describe your worth?
With what comparisons? No sun, no sky,
Nor any worshipped wonder on the Earth
Can match a single glimmer in your eye.
If Spring itself were multiplied by two,
It would not measure nearly half as much
As half a silent second spent with you;
As half your goodnight kiss, your gentle touch.
No, I'll not sit and foolishly appraise
Your value as I would some precious stone.
I'll not compare you in these common ways,
But liken you unto yourself alone.
The answer then is easier to give:
Your worth to me is every day you live.

AGAIN THE GEESE

BY JOEL ROGOSIN

it's Fall, the geese have come again
and I remember where and when
they came to stay and nest each year
then all too soon they'd disappear . . .
we watched and waited every day
certain that they'd find their way
so graceful, flying up so high
their numbers darkening the sky
we wondered where they always went
we knew that surely they'd been sent
to teach us tunes on whirring wings
and show their Vs stretched out like strings . . .
the months pass slowly when you're young
with camp songs often left unsung
and patience is a lot to bear
with few adventures left to share . . .
but soon we knew the time had come
the subtle clues came one by one
we woke up early, watched the sky
hoping geese would soon fly by
returning to their homes at last
exhausted, flying far and fast . . .

and then when it was least expected
the geese arrived, still unprotected
and settling in, they stayed awhile
with dignity and grace and style . . .
the years pass slowly when you're old
embracing fire, withstanding cold
but even so, the flock still comes
it's possible, the very ones
I waited for when I was young
the taste of Winter on my tongue
and all the girls were fair and game
to welcome back the geese again . . .

LUST FOR LIFE

I found a colored pencil sketch in my mother's trunk along with the baby shoes my brother and I both wore in their natural leather state among other treasures she kept until she died. The sketch was a portrait of my early childhood pet parakeet. I thought it was surprisingly good for a child to have done looking at it after all these years.

I don't remember when I began to love drawing and painting. Probably in kindergarten. I do remember that I looked forward to art classes and workshops whenever and wherever I could find them throughout most of my life.

When I discovered and fell in love with watercolor, I found it a natural fit with my love of wildlife and it was a place I seldom veered very far from.

The dream of any sort of gainful employment in art was extinguished when I took a class in design at LACC and realized I didn't have what it takes and after being rejected by Disney (I thought that painting cells was just staying within the lines and I could do that) but they weren't into letting me work there even in an office job so I sought work in live entertainment just to be near where art was being made although in a different creative realm.

But I continued doing what might be called painting just for me and it remained my favorite pastime. It is still the only hobby that I've ever had that I got so absorbed in that I lost track of time and forgot to eat. Eating is a very close second favorite pastime.

—Shirley Cohen

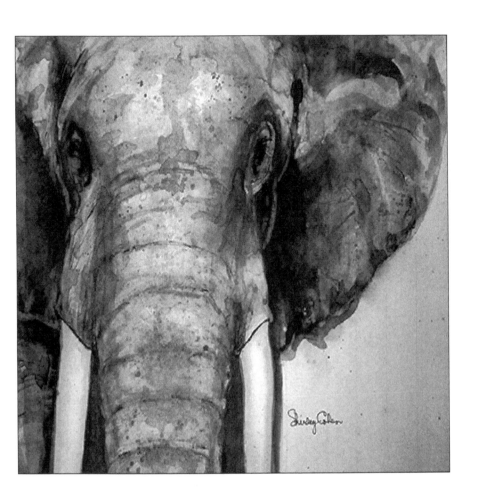

Shirley Coten '00

FEAR AND DESIRE

I AM HERE

BY ANTHONY LAWRENCE

When H. G. Wells wrote his speculative novel, *The Invisible Man* back at the end of the nineteenth century, he seemed more interested in the scientific probabilities of his fantasy than its philosophical questions.

He made every effort to make his story plausible, but the metaphorical implications of the protagonist and his dilemma are interesting to explore. After all, if there is a God, then we are all sons and daughters of "The Invisible Man."

We were invisible before we got here and we will become invisible when our days here are finished.

From the dawn of time, humankind has struggled against the fear of mortality. Our need to have mattered, to leave some trace of our existence can be seen through the paintings on the walls of caves.

We have given form and substance to our gods, to our dreams, and we have, through art, music, and literature, used our imaginations to leave exquisite evidence of who and what we are, as if possessed by the desire to prove to alien beings that we have been here and were of great consequence.

There seems to be an existential drive within each human that opposes a hostile environment and inevitable invisibility.

Animals have an instinct for survival. They just don't seem to care in one way or the other about the nature of existence. But human ego, the built-in forces of evolution and our own survival instincts make us determined, above all else, to see and be seen throughout our time here. We have even imagined all kinds of afterlives, Heavens and Valhallas, to extend our stays beyond the plainly visible.

But there is much more than the simple fact of "seeing" and "being seen" than our physical presence. It is in the ultimate and intimate way that humans communicate with one another, through the five senses of sight, sound, touch, smell, and taste that we are truly visible.

Really "being here" is in making contact with others; this is how we oppose invisibility.

Modern technology recognizes this as it continually strives to improve methods of communication, ever miniaturizing the already small microchip and transistor down toward a useful microscopic nanotechnology. E-mail, Facebook, Twitter, these are all the means by which we are determined to declare our visibility and existence to others.

But the prime and primal way in which we make contact with all our senses is in how we have done it since the beginning of time; human sexuality, making love while being in love is still the most totally collaborative and gratifying of any of the many ways in which we make contact and validate our being. It is through love that we truly oppose invisibility.

There are those who have always believed that human sexual contact is solely for the purpose of procreation, and some believe that it is simply there for those who love each other to use as they see fit. But the truth is really to deny isolation and to make supreme contact with another of our species and thereby to express the most important of all human endeavors, to cry out to our own kind, to others, and to the gods, "I am here."

SING BABY SING

BY DAVID KRAMER

There were nine singers in my family if you counted my cousin Terry, who was Stan Kenton's first vocalist. She was Rosie's daughter. Mama herself was a blues shouter. Six sisters were Selma (who sang opera) and the five famed Locust Sisters. The latter were vaudeville stars who later were on Broadway, in the musical short films of MGM, and did limited tours of nightclubs in large cities.

Decades passed without even a demisemiquaver sneaking from my lips, until my sixtieth year, when my wife, Gabi and I were on a business trip to Washington, D.C. We always stayed at the Hay Adams because they had a small dance floor and a gifted pianist playing Broadway tunes and pop songs from my era as we danced. Absentmindedly, I began humming the tune in my wife's ear, and within minutes I was actually crooning the lyrics. Gabi froze. I stepped back to see her face, which was in shock. "How is it that we've been married five years, and I never knew you had a great singing voice?"

"Because I never knew until this second, myself!"

Once the shock wore off, I figured that my voice had matured, but I never sang to anybody else. After all, my wife loved me. Anyone else? Ehhh—not so sure. But I sang frequently to her, and then she died, and I thought my voice went with her.

IT'S AWFUL

BY LISABETH HUSH

It's awful that woman passes
So much envy about herself
It bounds off her in icicle
Verbal displays by desperate
Aging young men
Who want the right to feel
&
Feel right only when
They bash their skulls
Because endless curiosity
Rocks their fucked bodies
&
Celebrate ritual misery
In each cellular hollow . . .

What must it be like
To want to be a woman
So much u get an operation
To be one
&
You still don't know
But now u know you were
Mad to think u could kno
&

To do what u did 2 kno
&
So were they who said
They would operate
&
Those who said "I told u so . . . "
But most of all, those of either
Sex who said "I already know."

SHERRI

BY DEBORAH ROGOSIN

My five clients that day included a new one named Sherri, who was coming in first at ten o'clock. She had been very reticent on the telephone and didn't want to answer any of my questions until she saw me in person.

She arrived about five minutes early, and I had her wait a few minutes so she could get her bearings and relax a little. As I invited her into the office, she looked to me about twenty-eight or thirty, very petite, quite pretty, but extremely intense. For a few minutes, she just sat and looked at me. I told her she must have something very serious on her mind. Sherri started sobbing. I walked over and sat next to her on the couch and put my arm around her shoulders. She leaned towards me and her sobbing increased. I tried to calm her and finally asked what was bothering her the most, knowing that she was likely carrying a host of problems with her.

She collected herself and said, "I've been lying to my husband!" Then, "I guess I haven't really lied, I just haven't written to him and told him the truth. He's away, in the army."

"That must be very difficult for you," I said. "Tell me what you haven't told him. It will be our secret."

She finally began to tell her story. During the past Christmas season, she had been shopping for her two small children, ages two and five, after leaving them with her sister at home. She walked out of a department store in the Northridge Mall and headed for her car when a man stepped beside her and pressed something into her side.

"I have a gun under my coat. Feel it? You're coming with me." She didn't know whether to scream or faint or what to do. He was holding her arm tightly and she couldn't believe this was happening to her. There were people around. She deliberately dropped her packages. He quickly and matter-of-factly picked them up and handed them back. "Nothing like that again, understand?" said he, and then prodded her with the gun as he walked her across the parking lot and put her into the passenger seat of an old green panel truck. He took the gun out of his pocket, put it on the dashboard in front of her, and quickly tied her hands and feet with a length of clothesline stashed on the floor. He was efficient and even thoughtful as he fastened her safety belt and closed the door, locking it.

He then recovered his gun and walked around to the driver's side of the car. As people came and went and cars pulled out, heading home for dinner, Sherri wanted to call out, but she bit her lip as he drove away into the traffic.

They drove around for about twenty minutes, but it seemed like an hour. All the time he was telling her she was going to have the time of her life with him, and for a moment he exposed himself as if to prove it. This would either be her greatest day, he said, or her last. She told him she had a husband and two little ones waiting for her to come home and fix dinner. Actually, her husband had been sent to Desert Storm, but she certainly didn't want to tell him that.

As she told me her story, Sherri was dabbing at her eyes with the tissues I'd given her. But she seemed much more in control as she told me her story, even as she seemed to relive it.

The man drove through an alley and into a garage, maybe in Van Nuys or Reseda, she thought, noticing the turns he made. She felt feelings of panic sweeping over her and thought about her babies with no Mommy.

The man carried her from the garage into the house, into a bedroom, and threw her on the bed. He untied her, but then retied each of her hands and feet to the four corners of the bed with the straps that were attached, not bothering to take her clothes off. He asked if she wanted to watch or be blindfolded.

She thought of something then and told him she was in the middle of her period. His smile was like ice. "So what?" he said. He untied one leg and slid her panties down. Then he raped her. When she moved her hips, trying to elude him, it only aroused him further. She kept trying to think of other things, willing herself to not be there on the bed with him.

She determined to remember every detail, so she could assist in his capture when he let her go . . . if he let her go.

He was a brutish looking and overweight man, maybe forty or fifty years old, and he smelled of disgusting body odor and cigarettes. The room looked gray and grubby. He took his time, breathing hard and sweating profusely. But there was something . . . compelling about him. At last, he was finished and he rolled off of her. Then, he got her purse and went through it, reading her address aloud and taking all the cash she had out of her wallet. He then took her watch and rings. She thought he would take her earrings, too, if her hair had not been covering them.

She asked him if she could go now, but he told her he wasn't finished having fun. *Oh God*, she thought to herself, how could she get away from him. After pondering for a few minutes, she asked if she could go to the bathroom.

He said, "I don't know about that," but she finally convinced him she really had to go very badly and she didn't want to dirty his bed. Besides, she had to clean herself up.

He untied her hands and dragged her into the bathroom and sat her on the toilet seat. She asked if she could have a glass of water, and to please shut the door, which he refused to do, but he offered to stand out in the hallway and not look at her. As he went out, she managed to kick the door shut and lock it.

She glanced at the sink where she saw a razor, grabbed it and started sawing at the rope, cutting through quickly. She climbed up on the counter and opened the window, then as quietly as possible scrambled through, dropping to the ground. She could hear the man calling, banging on the door. She ran to a neighbor's house, climbed over a wall, and behind the wall in the bushes, she finally relieved herself.

I suggested we take a break, but she was eager to go on, to finish her story. I reminded her that we had been talking about the lie that she did or did not tell her husband. I was beginning to get an idea of what this was really all about. Of course, it had nothing to do with telling him or not telling him about the rape—but with handling the guilt of what she didn't say: part of her actually enjoyed it. She wasn't ready to face that truth today. She didn't realize it until months later.

The man ran out of the house, looking for her. He went to the alley, looked over both fences and went to the neighbor's front door. Sherri went out the back gate, shutting it very quietly, and climbed the fence across the alley just before the two men—he and his neighbor—opened the back door and walked through the yard, looking under bushes.

It was getting darker and colder, so she quietly waited inside another neighbor's garage, cutting off the rest of the rope on one leg. Oh, if only her husband were here!

After a while, she made a plan. Since she was in the Valley, she knew there were main streets every few blocks. She went through a neighbor's yard to move to the next block when a little dog started to bark. She fell on the ground and started calling the dog, "Baby, come here, you sweet baby". The dog started to wag his tail and stopped barking. She sat there for a few minutes and cuddled the dog. Then she walked the alleys for a few blocks, hiding behind garbage cans each time a car approached.

Thank God, the kids are at my sister's house! We can't go home again with that horrible despicable man knowing where I live! Then, she saw a sign that said Sepulveda Boulevard and made a mental note of the name of the cross street. She saw a gas station a block away. She went to the attendant, a young man, and told him she had been robbed and could she please use his phone to call the police and her family. She immediately dialed 911. The attendant was very obliging and even offered to take her home but she decided to wait for the patrol car.

Just then the man in the green panel truck drove into the gas station. Sheri dropped to the floor, hiding. The young man saw her and asked her if she was all right. She said, yes, she just didn't want to be seen.

The young man shouted towards the green car, "I'll be right with you, Dad."

FUTURE IMPERFECT

BY MICHAEL REAVES

Earth may be the cradle of humanity, but one cannot live forever in a cradle.

—Konstantin Tsiolkovsky

It may already be too late. (At least no one's accused me of burying the lead.)

According to entirely too many grim meteorological predictions made by entirely too many grim-faced meteorologists, even if we stop all greenhouse emissions now, the sheer inertia of the planetary weather system will cause Earth's average surface temperature to rise dramatically according to the Intergovernmental Panel on Climate Change. It seems that the 21st Century is playing host to all four Horsemen, only they're wearing Armani and riding SUVs.

Maybe the increasing gradient won't be a tipping point that'll cause a runaway greenhouse effect, ending in Earth becoming another Venus in a hundred million years or so. But it will cause rampant desertification, wholesale die-offs of sea life due to acidification, catastrophic rises in ocean levels, a supply crisis in potable water— and that's not in some dim and murky distant future; that's in your lifetime, if you're in your twenties. But we have to profoundly change the way we look at the future, and, considering the train wreck that is the current administration, the role that we play in it.

We have to start thinking in terms of Deep Time.

Robert A. Heinlein famously said, "Earth is too small a basket for mankind to keep all its eggs in." Too true. Sooner or later we're going to be pulverized by a killer asteroid, or fried by a super-volcano, or pulsed by an EMP from a solar flare, or . . . pick any one of a dozen potential apocalypses.

The most discussed and scariest concept for an ELE (Extinction Level Event) is the killer asteroid scenario (although I personally favor the super-volcano; there's nothing you can do if Yellowstone decides to blow its stack, whereas with an incoming asteroid you can at least lob a couple of space shuttles full of movie stars at it and hope for the best.) We'd best attach a rider to their pay-or-play deals chop-chop, however, because it could happen any time from within the next ten thousand centuries to—well, now. This isn't hyperbole. Consider, if you will, several bullet points (with the emphasis on "bullet"):

In 1990, an asteroid big enough to cause destruction comparable to Hiroshima's A-Bomb hit us. That's right. Hit. Us. It didn't make headlines because the impact was in the middle of the South Pacific, far enough from land that there was no tsunami effect. But a few hours either way would have had people talking. The ones that weren't busy ducking and covering, that is . . .

(For those of you into irony, this particular big ol' rock is also known as Asclepius, God of healing. I know, right?)

The year before that, Asteroid 1989FC missed us by six hours. The size of an aircraft carrier, if it had hit in water (the most likely scenario, given that seventy percent of Earth is covered with ocean) it would have caused a mega-tsunami; a wave at least three hundred times as powerful as the 2004 Asian Tsunami.

But we were tracking it, right? Had it in our crosshairs? Ready to blast it to smithereens with a killer laser beam? Dream on. We didn't have a clue. A bunch of techs looked at the plates later and said, "Wait, what?" It skimmed us closer than the tattooed swastika on a skinhead's scalp.

Scared? You should be.

Bottom line: Earth is a big, slow target. And one thing we all learned from dodgeball is that it's better to be small and light on your feet—and, if you can manage it, in several places at once.

The best way to survive is to get some of us, at least, the hell out of Dodge. The problem is that leaving is far easier said than done. We've got two obstacles that are, by any reasonable definition, insurmountable.

The first is distance. The only world other than Earth that we've visited so far is the moon, and it's the only one we're likely to visit again anytime soon. That's right; you might as well stuff any notions of reaching other star systems, including ones relatively "close by," back in your tinfoil-lined fedora, because even with the fastest rocket propulsion currently available, travel to the closest stars will still take millennia. Proxima Centauri, the next star over, is four and a half light years away, the interstellar equivalent of down the street and around the corner. Doesn't sound too bad—until you remember that a light year is six trillion miles. Do the math on that one (hint: one trillion is one followed by twelve zeroes) and you'll get a vague inkling of the distances out there. Which means that some über-geek with coke-bottle glasses had better come up with warp drive in his parents' basement soon because there's no way we're crossing the cosmos in first gear.

So let's consider our satellite. While it's close enough to make round trips semi-practical, it ain't exactly a garden spot. Could we set up a permanent colony there? Frankly, I doubt it. We barely have people living full-time and raising families at the South Pole, and it's Cancun compared to the moon. With temperature extremes that range over five hundred degrees in a single step from sunlight to shade, an atmosphere less than one-trillionth that of Earth's, and worst of all, an omnipresent and highly-toxic layer of pulverized meteorite dust that, once through the airlock and into your lungs, can cause pneumoconiosis faster than you can cough up blood, the moon doesn't seem anybody's first choice for prime extraterrestrial real estate.

But—location, location, location, remember? The one thing we can count on is that the moon will always be about the same drive time. Which is a lot more than we can say about the only other halfway habitable rock in the inner system: Mars. That's because while the moon is tucked away, nice and snug, in orbit around the Earth, Mars and Earth both orbit the sun—and Mars's orbit is a lot more eccentric. A lot. Mars can be anywhere from thirty-six million miles to over 250 million miles from us. In travel time that works out to anywhere from half a year to a year and a half, which makes booking rooms in advance a real bitch.

Trouble is, it's the best alternative of all the other planets. Mercury? Like the moon, only hotter. Venus? Pretty to look at, but underneath those clouds the surface makes Hell seem hospitable; it's the hottest place in the Solar System, outside of Sol itself. (Although there are extenuating circumstances in the case of Venus; more on this later.) How about the outer worlds—Jupiter, Saturn, Uranus, Neptune? They're not called "gas giants" out of sophomoric frat-house humor; there's no "there" there, no hard and fast boundary between lithosphere and atmosphere. And let's not bother mentioning Pluto; it's not even officially a planet anymore.

Even if there were some place in the Outer Planets that was halfway habitable, the gas giants and their moons are so far away that they might as well be in another solar system. Grad students lost cherries and gained doctorates during the decade and more it took the New Horizons probe to reach Pluto. And that expedition was only feasible because the onboard robot had no need for life-support. There's no way we can afford to send crewed exploratory flights on a three billion mile schlep. The amount of food and fuel needed makes it impossible to get a manned mission of that complexity off the ground. Not to mention water. It's true that recycling from sources best left unnamed can maximize usage, but eventually, the stores have to be replenished. While there is water on the moon, as well as the moons of the ice giants, there isn't enough to warrant establishing full-time colonies that far out. Mars, on the other hand, has plenty of subsurface water, but again, the ratio of H_2O to the energy required to land and dig for it is problematic.

Still, it looks like, for all its considerable drawbacks—temperatures that only look good compared to the moon, the lack

"It sparked the beginning of a decade-long, across-the-board effort. . . . to win the Cold War by beating the godless Commies to the moon. Because make no mistake; we needed a foe, a mysterious and implacable enemy to rally the troops so that, on that glorious day in July 1969, we could stand proud as a nation on the dusty gray plain of Mare Tranquilatis and say to the Soviets in a voice strong and united: "Neener-neener-neener!"

of a magnetosphere, which makes a tan deadly, and a travel time about twice as long as sailing around Cape Horn (along with enough cosmic rays to give the entire population of Detroit superpowers)—Mars is the best place.

Except . . . remember I said two obstacles?

Space is big—there's no getting around that. But as staggeringly complex as merely getting to another world is, there's a much greater problem once we're there. One which makes cosmic rays, temperature extremes and lack of atmosphere look easy. We can overcome these problems, at least in theory, with terraforming techniques. It would require decades of engineering on a cosmic scale—playing planetary billiards with icy comets to create oceans, putting orbital mirrors up to magnify sunlight, using hydroponics to "grow" oxygen and nitrogen. Given decades of global restructuring, Mars could be tricked out with a breathable atmosphere, a decent climate—everything except one essential thing:

Gravity. That's the one thing we can't increase or decrease since it's a function of mass. Mars is one-third the size of Earth and has (more or less) one-third as much gravity. The moon has one-sixth. And we won't be changing either one any time in the near future. So, unless we're lucky enough to find a Counter-Earth tucked away on the other side of the sun whose gravitational pull is within ten to twenty percent, plus or minus, of Earth's (hint: we won't), we're screwed.

The problem is that, no matter how many technological advances we make, genetically we're still just a bunch of hairless apes jabbing each other with pointed sticks on the African veldt. We evolved in a one gravity field, and when we spend prolonged periods out of it (such as a few months up in the space station), bad things happen.

How bad?

Real bad.

Prolonged weightlessness causes, among other things, dehydration, musculoskeletal atrophy, anemia, mineral and electrolyte depletion, vertigo, and a whole host of other problems ranging from unpleasant to downright life-threatening. Back in the "Pulp Era" of science fiction, when space flight was still a testosterone-fueled dream, it was theorized that time spent in zero-gee would actually be good for the body. No stress on the joints or the heart would logically mean no wear and tear on other moving parts; ergo, you might outlive Methuselah and remain as spry as Barishnakov.

Unfortunately, like so many rose-colored visions of The Future everyone had back then, pretty much the opposite holds true. Long-term weightlessness resembles, in syndrome, accelerated aging. Spend a couple of years in space (the average time of a trip to Mars), and you wind up looking—and feeling—like your grandfather. Sure, the process can be slowed somewhat—by near-constant workouts. I don't know about you, but riding an Exercycle all the way to the Red Planet and back isn't a trip I'm particularly looking forward to.

And we haven't even discussed the physical and psychological effects (about which, admittedly, we don't know much yet, but the probabilities aren't looking good) of carrying a child to term and raising him or her in a lighter gravitational field. How will nine months in a womb on Mars affect bone structure? Muscle development? Brain growth? We don't know . . . but I'm not exactly going out on a galactic spiral arm here by guessing it won't be good.

And on top of all that, the latest findings indicate quite strongly that combined solar and galactic high-energy cosmic rays, zapping through the inner and outer planetary neighborhoods with a reckless abandon that would make a Bangladeshi traffic cop's jaw hit the asphalt like Wile E. Coyote's, are several orders of magnitude more dangerous than previously expected. So, in addition to the dangers already listed in our Martian odyssey, we can add making the trip in what is essentially an enormous microwave oven.

Doesn't look good, does it? Earth's on a fast track to disaster, the only other worlds we have even the faintest chance of reaching aren't even remotely pleasant, and just getting there can kill us. And there's no other world within practical reach—certainly not in the next century or so, which everybody with a Ph.D. is telling us is longer than we've got left here.

So what can we do?

We can make a world.

Gravity is far and away the weakest force in the universe. Hard to believe, but true—the electromagnetic energy contained in a refrigerator magnet weighing a quarter of an ounce is more than sufficient to overcome the gravitational energy of the entire Earth—which weighs, in case you're interested, six septillion metric tons, give or take a few million. (Actually, the Earth doesn't weigh anything, technically, since it's in a state of constant free fall around the sun.)

But while gravity is weak, it's also pervasive. Although it decreases with distance, it never fades completely; the upshot being that the gravitational forces from the sun, the moon, Earth and the other planets all interact, creating whorls and eddies in spacetime like colliding river currents in a placid lake.

These result in stable spots at certain locations called LaGrange Points: areas of space where the orbits of celestial bodies balance with gravitational forces. There are five of them in the Earth-Moon system alone, and the L-4 and L-5 points are so stable that large objects, plunked down in the middle of them will stay there, without course corrections, for a long, long time.

Gravity's not a problem either. If you're living on the inside of a cylinder instead of on the surface of a planet, it's easy (well, easier) to create "artificial gravity" by simply spinning the cylinder. Centrifugal Force pushes everything against the inner surface of the torus, just like in those old Tilt-A-Whirl rides at the carnival. It isn't a force in the classical sense; merely a moving body's resistance to a change in inertia. It's a "phony force" instead of a real one, like centripetal force, but who cares? The point is that the effect is indistinguishable from gravity. And if the cylinder big enough, the inner-ear effect will be diluted, so you won't constantly feel like throwing up everything you've eaten since you were five. (There's also an impressive variety of antiemetic drugs available OTC to settle that queasy tummy.)

What's more, the LaGrange Points aren't just confined to the Earth-Moon system—there are points of stability everywhere that planets and moons do their complex orbital dances. Colonies built at these libration points are the only viable way of leaving Earth behind. Controlled environments, with regulated day and night cycles, normal "gravity," free from natural disasters such as volcanos, floods, and earthquakes, and presenting much smaller, faster-moving targets for giant impactors, make a helluva lot more sense than trying to hardscrabble a living on the moon or Mars.

It's also possible to build "gravity wheels"—essentially enormous centrifuges desired to take up the inertial slack, though it would probably take as long, and in the case of Mars at least, cost as much or more to build a habitat in orbit than it would on the planet's surface, once you factor in the extra distance and the mining of raw materials. It's cheaper and easier to use metals and ores from near-Earth asteroids that are "low-hanging fruit" and take advantage of the much finer production quality of zero-gee metallurgy, not to mention the vastly shorter commute. Besides, the quality of life possible in a habitat is limited only by architectural imagination, whereas once you've finished construction of a base on Mars you still have to deal with problems ranging from the niggling, such as that extra forty minutes in each Martian day, to the life-threatening planetary dust storms. Not to mention It—the Terror From Beyond Space.

I trust I've made my point . . .

And for those who find the nonstop carney ride too much, take heart! There's even a way to have your gravity and mass too ("mass" refers, in this case, to an object's resistance to acceleration, not a liturgy.) I'm referring to a summer home on Venus.

Huh?

Hear me out, okay? It's true that living on Venus is tantamount to living in a deep fat fryer. But I'm not pitching that. There's more to the planet than just the surface. Around 90 klicks straight up there's a gap in the clouds. The temperature levels out to around 35°C—which is shirtsleeve weather, as long as one wears an oxygen mask or stays in the big gondolas that would keep the population protected.

In 1950, the physicist Enrico Fermi ruined everyone's lunch by asking one of the most troublesome rhetorical questions in astrophysics:

"Where is everybody?"

I'm talking helium balloons, just like Montpelier used to make, only considerably bigger.

Best of all, Venus has very nearly the same mass—which this time means the same gravity—as Earth. It's true that a somewhat depressing sameness of cloud cover dominates the scene, but it's better in just about every other way. The gravity is real gravity, not the ersatz version you get under the big tent. And yes, it's true that the Venerian magnetosphere isn't nearly as strong as Earth's—but it's stronger than Mars's, which is zero, zip, nada—y'know, zilch.

And eventually, once we settle in all nice and comfy, we can build smaller, sleeker craft with solar sails or other passive propulsion devices that'll take our descendants to the Centauri system, or Barnard's Star, or other "local" systems. Long before then, we'll have space-based telescopes powerful enough to ascertain which stars have Earth-like worlds—although our heirs will, in all probability, think it insane to leave our comfortable climate-controlled habitats to return to the chaos of a planetary environment. After all, would you seriously consider abandoning the air-conditioned environment of your condo for a damp and dank cave?

In August of 1962, President John F. Kennedy asked rhetorically, Why choose to go to the moon? "We choose to go to the moon," he said, "in this decade and do the other things, not because they are easy, but because they are hard. Because that goal will serve to organize and measure the best of our energies and skills, because that challenge is one that we are willing to accept, one we are unwilling to postpone, and one which we intend to win."

With those words, the thirty-fifth President sounded a clarion call that defined the Sixties for as many or more than the war in Viet Nam, the music of the Doors, or the art of R. Crumb. It sparked the beginning of a decade-long, across-the-board effort that united scientists, teachers, engineers, doctors, test pilots (the last group under the new rubric of "astronauts") and many others in a single goal—to win the Cold War by beating the godless Commies to the moon. Because make no mistake; we needed a foe, a mysterious and implacable enemy to rally the troops so that, on that glorious day in July 1969, we could stand proud as a nation on the dusty gray plain of Mare Tranquilatis and say to the Soviets in a voice strong and united: "Neener-neener-neener!"

Many felt that America's military, engineering and scientific communities have never been as unified regarding anything as we were behind the space program during those ten years—despite the generation gap, burning bras and draft cards, and a distressing tendency on the part of circuit court judges to throw beardless youths into hardcore maximum security for a few decades just for possession of a single Jamaican Red joint. (On the other hand, it was Christmas all year long for inmates named Bubba and Cletus.)

To reach the moon, we crammed fifty years of technological development into a single decade. It won't be as easy this time. This time our foe can't be found in the gray monolithic hallways of the Kremlin or the Forbidden City. This time, as Walt Kelly's Pogo said, "We have met the enemy and he is us."

Which brings us back to Deep Time.

Instead of going for the quick fix, the (relatively) easy gratification, we'll have to adopt a mindset that we as a species haven't used for centuries: patience. We have to look back in order to move forward; back to the times when the human race routinely embarked on projects so monumental, they took generations to finish. Projects like the cathedrals of Europe, the pyramids of Egypt, the ziggurats of Meso-America and the aqueducts of Rome; projects of which the builders knew they would never see the completion. The trade-off was a lifetime of room and board (if not necessarily pay).

It was easier for people who lived back then to accept that one's father and one's son would be employed on the same venture because back then the future looked much like the past. Change was slow and incremental; we hadn't reached the steep part of the roller-coaster yet, whereas today we've toiled up and over the top and are now in free-fall. Stop screaming and think of the world a hundred and fifty years ago: the majority of the population had never even heard the sound of an internal combustion engine nor seen an airplane, much less ridden in one. Most lived and died within fifty miles of their birthplace. The world's population was just over a billion, and life expectancy for adults in America around fifty. Since then, there have been more changes—technologically, biologically, sociologically, or in any other venue you can name—in the twentieth century than in all of human history.

And as for the twenty-first century:

"We set sail on this new sea because there is new knowledge to be gained, and new rights to be won, and they must be won and used for the progress of all people."

The stakes are far higher than Kennedy knew; far, far higher than few today will admit. Because what's at stake now isn't just progress—it's survival. If humanity is going to make it, it won't be here on planet Earth. It'll be out there: outside the atmosphere, beyond the van Allen Belts, across the frothing sea of radiation and cosmic dust.

And the diaspora will be soon. How do I know this?

Because if it isn't accomplished soon, humanity is done.

But we don't have to be. We have most of the technology we need—in fact, we are far better equipped and prepared to create the L-5 habitats and the floating cloud cities of Venus with our current level of knowledge and ability than we were capable of landing a man on the moon a decade prior to Neil Armstrong's one small step.

It's our choice. Oh, sure, we can wait for the aliens to come, arriving against a background of theremin music and a strobing light show, and just give us the tech we need. But the chances of it coming from star-folk sporting heads the size of casaba melons and Seventies-style silver lamé jumpsuits? Put it this way:

In 1950, the physicist Enrico Fermi ruined everyone's lunch by asking one of the most troublesome rhetorical questions in astrophysics: "Where is everybody?"

The Fermi Paradox, as it came to be known, is simply stated: it cites the apparent contradiction between the high probability of extraterrestrial civilizations' existence and the lack of contact with them. According to the Drake Equation, it seems probable that many extra-terrestrial civilizations are ephemeral; if they form at all, they don't last very long. And that's the problem. Despite the unimaginable distances between the stars, what isolates us isn't space so much as time. Consider: Homo sapiens has only been around for a half million years, and we've only been broadcasting our presence for a hundred or so. And, after a brief spike in the fifties and sixties, our radio wave transmissions have fallen off sharply in recent years, because everyone's gotten cable. (Yeah, that's right; the chances of E.T. phoning us have dropped drastically because you had to have HBO.) Pop quiz, hotshot: given the billions of years it takes life to develop on worlds such as Earth, what are the odds of some aliens just happening to intercept a Jerry Lewis telethon on their interstellar iPhone by listening in at precisely the right cosmic moment?

Your answer counts for half your grade.

The paradox of the Great Silence has only grown more salient with the discovery in the last decade of a huge bevy of exoplanets. With literally billions of Earth-like worlds estimated in our galaxy alone, the chances are overwhelming that life must have developed on a significant portion of them, and intelligent life (if we define "intelligence" as the ability to imagine and eventually search for other civilizations) on at least a few. If no more than one other civilization made it further than we have, they could have seeded the entire galaxy with robot probes in a few million years. That sounds like a long stretch, but in terms of Deep Time, it's really not. The Milky Way is over ten billion years old; almost as old as the universe itself. A million years—a million centuries—is nothing.

Once SETI put its collective ear to the sky back in the early Sixties, we had every expectation of hearing radio waves from Out There buzzing, humming, stridulating and otherwise vocalizing juicy galactic gossip. Instead, we got the lonesome interstellar equivalent of crickets chirping.

But—even considering the few brief sparks of civilizations

guttering in the vast cosmic night, such a plenitude of Earth-like worlds postulated still begs Fermi's question: Where is everybody?

There are a few hypotheses as to where everybody's hiding—my favorite is the Prime Directive, a.k.a. the Zoo Hypothesis, which should be self-explanatory even to non-Trekkies. But there's also a more sinister one, known as the Great Filter. It says that the majority of civilizations reach a point at which they either run out of energy and catastrophically return to barbarism, or make it past the crisis and enter a technological utopia.

Judging from the signal-to-noise ratio out there, it would seem that utopia is seldom achieved.

But "seldom" isn't the same as "never." I think that, if we want to join the galactic Kiwanis, we'll have to take the initiative.

We have to get the hell out of Dodge.

Imagine a future a hundred years from now: a huge factory station, one of dozens set in orbit around a big ol' asteroid where robot miners feed a constant supply of raw materials to us, to be fabricated into whatever we desire. It's certainly a pleasant vision of the centuries to come—far more so than endless variations of Little House On Valles Marineris. And we'll have the luxury of time to decide if it's for us or not. Time and space, and plenty of both.

All of eternity and infinity.

Mankind has searched for a way to secure passage into Heaven (without the inconvenient proviso of having to die first), for as long as he's walked upright. Prayer hasn't proven overly efficacious—neither have sacrifices or genocide. But now, finally, we have the tools; if we have the will and the fortitude as well, we can build Heaven.

It's that, or take our chances on an Earth that's all too rapidly going to Hell.

LOVER

BY LISABETH HUSH

He's known as a lover
But not as a mate
Simpleton, he hates us
He leaves us so soon
Staring-and-starting inside
              His own skull/
His body forgets us so quickly
                 We go
And another he gathers
And another lets go/

He tells you he's fine
As
He preaches by phone—
(I've never seen such misery
           Unless it is my own)/

He envies all us women
As he sits at home alone
Making up his poetry,
Waiting for his call from
Yet another woman
Who hasn't learned the scent
Of a man whose passion ends
When he's got his food
           And rent/

Pretty little thing,
Nervous as a cat
Jumps on a female
Performs his manly act
Lets her buy the butter
Make the tea
Drive him somewhere
               Walk back/

There's always one more
               Woman
To sidle to this sphinx
I'd like to catch him screaming
And
Tie him to his bed
Past when he wants his loving
Past the last scream inside his head—
I think that then he'd love me
Tell me I'm the best of all,
That he wanted to be captured
That he feels at home in jail//

PRESCRIPTION

BY WILLIAM BLINN

I usually enjoy looking down at the flat Midwestern plains, finding strength there in the neatly manicured fields, the green and brown, the tented fall wardrobe offing a solidity I could not find in the West Coast carousel. I found none of that solid strength today looking down from United Flight 445, Los Angeles to Akron. My sister's phone call of last night had drained all strength from the equation.

"Sweetie, Mom's had a stroke. The doctors say it's bad."

The engine changed pitch as the plane started to lose altitude. I leaned closer to the window as landmarks started to take shape below. The high school. The field house. My Uncle Ned's garage supply warehouse. The water tower, red light blinking on top. Crisscrossing gray concrete runways. A couple of Pipers warming up prior to taking flight. There was a low mechanical groan as the landing gear came down. A sharp bird-chirp when the tire bit the landing strip. A song lyric came bubbling up.

Home again, home again. Johnny's so late at the fair.

Shirley told me the events of the last night with as much level-headed calm as she could manage. She was in the front seat with her oldest daughter, Kerry. It had been three weeks since Kerry had attained her driver's license. Kerry drove with hyper-caution. This did not stop Shirley from offering a nonstop blur of instructions. "Stop sign, Kerry. Stop sign." "Too fast, baby girl. Too fast. That's better." Daughter Kerry stared straight ahead. Her jaws worked and worked.

As we headed for the hospital, Shirley told me of the sad events of the previous night. It was a Thursday, so she had gone over to pick Mom up for choir practice. Then there was Mom, motionless on the kitchen floor. The siren screaming ambulance ride to St. Vincent's

Memorial. Room 32. The dark prognosis from the medic. At this point, Kerry started to cry.

"Grandma won't be able to see me in the junior play." She sniffed a cargo of snot.

"Kerry, this is not about Grandma's not seeing you in the junior play."

"Well, then, what is it about?"

"It's about whether or not Grandma lives or dies, dammit!"

Another snot snort.

Shirley called and got me a room at the Dew Drop. I was to go see Mom and then get a cab from St. Vincent's. We would have breakfast at the Dew Drop coffee shop and then see what our next step ought to be. Kerry could not join us as she had a divisional soccer match that morning.

St. Vincent's was filled with hospital odors unknown to Dr. Kildare. Some of the hospital room doors stood open. The sallow faces on the beige pillows offered no encouragement. I was glad I had agreed to the reservation at the Dew Drop. There was a bar just off the lobby there.

Mom's complexion was the color of canned tuna. There was an IV inserted into the top of her hand. The blinking light of the cardiac monitor looked like the scarlet beacon atop the water tower at the airport. I stood at the foot of her hospital bed looking down on her, on my Mom. There was a time before when she had been on a hospital bed, but she had not been motionless. That other time she had been writhing and crying out with the effort needed to shove me out of her warmth and into the chill of the sharp-edged world in which I was meant to live. My hand curled hard about the cold metal of the bed frame. Then the door was opened behind me.

The doctor's name was Macomber, and he looked very tired. He introduced himself formally. His palm was velvet and moist. He explained what he could about my mom's condition. I listened politely and nodded as if I actually understood. I asked him if there was anything I could do. He shrugged. I hated him for that.

My mom deserved more than a shrug. He moved to the door. One hand lifted and took a soft grip on the knob. "You might try talking to her," he said.

My expression revealed my confusion.

"There's a school of thought," he said, "that says the sense of hearing is the last to go. That speaking to the patient can trigger a reaction—speaking about happier times, better times. Might trigger something or other."

"Meaning?"

"Meaning we don't know," he said. "Might get them all the way back. Or maybe just partway. Or not at all." He nodded politely and opened the door all the way. "Nice to have met you," he said. And then was gone.

I stood at the side of Mom's bed for a long time, just stood there, listening. I was listening for the sound of my own voice, reeling off a litany of happier times, as Dr. Macomber had requested. Birthday celebrations and picnics at the lakefront. Times with the kids chasing fireflies, squealing with a crazed delight they might never know again in all their lives. And there would be songs, too, old songs whose melodies spanned sunsets and brought sweet tears from over the horizon. But that voice I waited for, my very own voice, that voice never arrived with those happier times.

The voice I waited for, my voice, was absent, gagged by the fear building within, that all the good times might only call back a feeble portion of Mom. One that could not speak with clarity or recall with certainty. My mother had given birth to a male child unable to confront her fading away. And surely the notion that her male baby boy could not be strong for her would kill her, indeed. Indeed it would.

I lifted the receiver off the hook and dialed my sister's number. The phone buzzed several times on the other end. I reached over and patted Mom's hand. I made an effort to think of happier times.

SHE WAS NOT ALONE

BY JOAN TANNEN

When I discovered I had atrial fibrillation I found myself in the hospital for two weeks while medical staff worked to get me stabilized. During that time I had many roommates. The first had many visitors during the day and went home the next morning; therefore, I had little contact with her. Before she was discharged that morning she did call the nurse for me when my blood pressure dropped very, very low, and I fell on the floor unconscious as I got up to go to the bathroom. The second was very friendly and pleasant, but was very noisy, even at 3:00 a.m. The third turned out to be in "the industry" in some sort of production capacity, so we became quite friendly. The last one shared the room with me the shortest length of time, but she touched me in a very, unexpected way.

I didn't get a chance to talk to her because when she moved into the room her family stayed with her right up until visiting hours came to an end. She was very quiet so I didn't want to intrude. I was under the impression, from what I overheard, was that she had cancer and some cardiology issues. We were each settling into the evening hours, preparing to go to sleep. The room was darkened and quiet. I was dozing lightly about midnight when she cried out.

She cried out movingly and with awe in her voice, "Father . . . Father . . . Oh, Father . . . and then she was quiet. I lay there mulling in my mind what she'd said. A while later a nurse came in to check on her. I heard the nurse cry out, "Oh, my God!" She hurried out and soon three other nurses rushed in and out. The first nurse had called the family and a short while later the son arrived. As he wept over her body, he was allowed a long time to grieve. Another member of the family arrived to console him. Finally, he left and then the son left, his face swollen in sorrow.

Timidly, I wanted to reach out to him and reassure him that she had passed over very peacefully and, despite his fears that she was alone, she was not alone. But his face was so grief-stricken that I hesitated to intrude, and he passed my bed so quickly that I missed the opportunity.

When he left, the cadre of nurses moved in and swiftly and efficiently prepared her body to be transported from the room. They placed her in a body bag and lifted her body onto a gurney with built-up sides. The curtain was pulled so I couldn't see, but I could hear all their preparations. Finally, they placed sheets strategically around the sides of the gurney, so that she was completely hidden from view. It looked like what I imagined a funeral bier would look like. Then, very respectfully, they wheeled her out and down to the netherworld of the morgue. I had witnessed a very intimate and spiritual moment.

Is there an afterlife—a heaven? Do we really know?

HEAVEN CAN WAIT

MIRANDA

BY JOEL ROGOSIN

Miranda grew up with kittens and puppies and fragile songbirds, and over the years she found and rescued and adopted and raised and named them, and finally bid them goodbye with appropriate ceremony when their time came to "move away," as she called it.

Of course, there were people in her life she learned to love—her mother especially, who always seemed to understand even when there were no words. But it was the small, furry creatures she truly cherished, holding them warm and close so she could feel their heartbeats and share their breaths.

In appearance, she was clearly a woman, but always childlike because of the accident, which claimed both her parents and left her limited in some ways, desolate and alone. Taking care of the pets was her whole life.

When a man wanted to marry her, she agreed, with some idea of following her mother's wifely example. Eugene was much older and set in his ways, but he was kind to Miranda and he tolerated her pets in spite of fierce, debilitating allergies.

One day he fell ill, and one night soon after that he moved away. Miranda actually remembered him for a while. She had reluctantly neglected her furry friends while she cared for Eugene. Now, one by one, she found good homes for them with generous, loving families.

She kept three newborns for company—the spaniel puppies and the calico kitten. She didn't name them, knowing she'd have to part with them one day when they matured, but she was content for a while, playing with them and helping them grow.

Finally, she knew that she was older—old—and it was becoming more and more difficult for her to care for her precious companions—

feeding, grooming, visits to the vet. The calico cat was the last to go, to thirteen-year-old twins, and soon after Miranda began shutting herself up in her cottage, resigned to waiting as long as she had to until it was her time to move away.

She closed and shuttered one window at a time, then the doorway to the small, damp cellar where her mother had taught her to pickle beets in that other life, before the pets. After a while, she went up into the loft and lay on her mother's warm, cushiony bed, spreading her arms out to make "angel wings" in the covers like she'd been taught to do when it snowed, then falling asleep and dreaming of the little calico. Before they took her home, the twins had shared a secret with Miranda. They had named their brand new favorite pet Shortbread.

Time passed slowly for Miranda, who was virtually shut-in now and growing tired of waiting. When she brushed her teeth in the morning, she avoided looking into the bathroom mirror, inexplicably afraid of what she might see there. Once, her mother's reflection smiled back at her, or was it her own reflection, suddenly so like her mother's—thinning, wispy gray hair, pale blue eyes—laugh-lines, mostly for frowning now.

She was sipping tea-milk, as she'd often done with her mother, and dozing in the big bentwood rocker her husband had made for her, when the cluster of Christmas bells, hanging outside from a frayed red and green ribbon near the front door, suddenly rang. It was a sound she had rarely heard since her husband died, and it startled her. After a moment or two, she called out, her throat dry, her voice cracking. No answer. Slowly, she pulled herself up out of the rocker and ventured to the door.

It was stuck tight. She wrestled it open and stepped back, not comfortable looking at her visitor. Then she saw there was no one there. Glancing about, she noticed a small parcel on the splintered porch railing. Hesitantly, she picked it up, took it inside and closed the door.

It was a box, neatly wrapped in plain brown paper, with no identification or return address. Miranda settled herself in the rocker, holding the package in her lap, picking a little at a corner of the wrapper until she could tear it off neatly and fold it up to save in case someday she needed it.

The box was decorated with a picture of a life-like Maltese Terrier puppy, and as Miranda opened the box the puppy inside opened its eyes, blinked, and drew a breath. Surprised and delighted, Miranda reached in for it, holding it gently as it trembled a little in her hands. She calmed it with a whisper, stroking the soft fur, scratching the tiny spots behind the ears. The puppy licked her fingers and seemed to sigh contentedly as Miranda turned it over on her lap and tickled its belly.

There was a name on the box, which Miranda read out loud—RoboPet. She decided then and there to keep the puppy and call it Roby. There were other things written on the box—instructions and such—but Miranda was preoccupied with the wriggling ball of fur.

During the next few days, passersby, neighbors, and tradesmen noticed cottage windows open again, and sunlight playing on the walls inside, and there were glimpses of Miranda herself moving about. Among themselves, they spoke with relief about the welcome appearance of normalcy.

From time to time they saw Miranda outside, tending her garden or playing with her new puppy, watching it run around and around, laughing, holding her arms out to catch it when it jumped up on her.

When Miranda saw people looking, she smiled and waved, and some were invited in for tea-milk and homemade sugar cookies. The new puppy was always near, lying at her feet or dozing in her lap, its tail constantly in motion. It was a happy time, a good time, the best time Miranda could remember for being alive.

Then one day they found her, just like that, with a sweet, tender smile, as if asleep in her rocker—a frail, shrunken figure nearly lost among the big, fluffy pillows, the puppy resting quietly in her lap, its wagging tail finally stilled.

It was the twins who found her when they stopped by to show off their calico, Shortbread, full-grown now, and to find out if Miranda was enjoying the surprise package they'd left on the porch for her.

They knew at a glance that Miranda and her pup had both moved away. Now they'd always be off somewhere, romping together . . .

On the floor near the rocker, they spotted the box Roby had come in; the four triple-A "replacement batteries included" still scotch-taped and neglected inside.

IMPERFECTION AND IMPERMANENCE

BY SHIRLEY COHEN

Imperfection and impermanence—the twin sisters I live with but don't want to acknowledge, yet they are always with me. I can either learn to accommodate them or go on resisting them at my peril!

I recently caught the tail end of a discussion on TV having to do with "Imperfection and Impermanence." The phrase for some reason really resonated with me. I found that the phrase is a part of a traditional Japanese aesthetic called, *Wabi-Sabi*. It is centered on the acceptance of transience and imperfection, sometimes described as one of beauty that is "imperfect, impermanent, and incomplete. Nothing lasts, nothing is perfect. Accepting these hard facts opens the door to finding the beauty in old age, in a weathered character, focusing instead on the serenity that can come with time, when inevitable wear becomes a patina, and scars become signs of experience."

If only it were so easy for me to embrace *Wabi-Sabi*. But it's like a Koan to me, a Zen Buddhist riddle to demonstrate the inadequacy of logical reasoning. My naturally resistant mind resists opening the door!

As a child, the concept of death was the *most* frightening fact of life. In my childish mind, not being here anymore was inconceivable. With a little maturity, dealing with the passing of loved ones, death became more conceivable and more the reality of life's conclusion . . .

Now that coming to grips with the end of the road as it feels ever more close at hand, I'm not quite ready to "kiss today goodbye." It has been more comfortable to live in denial about the road dead-ending at some point down the highway but now the road signs begin to come into focus, signaling the warning: *prepare to stop, road ends in two miles!*

I find that in my own human frailty, I too often fail to take into consideration the human frailty of some of those around me. The fact that I'm not alone in this failure is of little consolation nor any excuse.

Even in these most perfect conditions, the people in the same boat, or bus in this mode of metaphoric transport, the—let's face it—*elderly*, and accepting that I'm one of them—dealing with this stage of life—I and others sometimes, without malice aforethought, unable to resist the impulse to lash out—for reasons known or maybe unknown only to ourselves. Maybe because of who we've become or perhaps never were.

Some of us often cannot hear or aren't listening, our words don't come, our fingers stiffen and kindness to ourselves and each other becomes difficult for some of us. Attaching to beautiful minds and souls who are here today and gone tomorrow, occurring with more frequency than in the world outside, and within such close proximity, sharpens my awareness of the reality taking shape.

Although I have begun to feel the decay of impermanence and the imperfection never resolved, I'm not ready to fade to black! It feels like—wait—have I ever really lived? Is it all a dream? Merrily rowing my boat down the stream . . . merrily or not, *is* life but a dream?

Someone once told me that they're going to write on my tombstone: "returned unopened!" That was said in jest and in reference to the fact that I held on to my virginity 'til I was practically elderly! But it has a certain ring of truth none the less.

The clichés and myths religion offers to inspire life or ease the way or forgive or punish sins and threaten the fires of hell or offer eternal bliss are yet another a Koan to me, another riddle of illogical reasoning and have little effect if any on my doubtful old soul.

The thought of an afterlife in heaven or continuous lives in the Karmic tradition would be wonderfully comforting if I could believe but I'm skeptical until someone comes back to tell about it . . .

Letting go of life as I've known it, would be easier to conceptualize if I felt that I had made the most of it. Up 'til now, I feel like

I haven't accomplished anything in my life to write home about. But I haven't, to echo Brett Hadley, "given up chasing the dream, no matter what." I am so grateful for the cheerleaders for living life in my world who make it all worthwhile and for the beautiful gardens in which to meditate, surrounded by "the wisdom of rocks and grasshoppers," thrilling to the songs of birds, the buzz of bees and hummers, going about their business, unaware of impermanence. Certainly unaware of imperfection, for they are perfect. And I am hopeful.

After chewing all this over, I'm sure there is still life to live and I hope it's not too late to create something worthy of memoir and something much better to put on my tombstone.

ISLAND

BY ANTHONY LAWRENCE

Once known as Hecate before rising
and after the black lamb goddess had set,
as Astarte when gibbous crescent,
or Cynthia who hunts the clouds
when in the open vault of heaven.

Like Phoebe when looked upon
as the sister of the sun,
or Luna on the fields, a triform sphere
waxing spiky horn toward the east,
or waning burnished salute
to face the west.

All that was treasured lies there,
things wasted on the earth,
misspent time and wealth,
broken vows and unanswered prayers,
fruitless tears and
unfulfilled desires.

Above the ebb and flow of persuaded tides,
in the mountains of the moon
bribes are hung on gold
and silver hooks; prince's favors
kept in bellows and wasted talent
in mammoth vases.

And the white opal island in velvet night,
when a single lustrous star pursues its tail,
becomes a man leaning on a fork
who carries a bundle of sticks
picked up on a Sunday, a man named Cain
with a foul dog and bush of thorns
that are briars of the fall.

DOG. A SHORT STORY

BY PHIL HABERMAN

Me and my friend Herby walked up to Riverside Park this morning. We go there often. We like it there. The city noise is gone. Just the sounds of the park. The Hudson River. Freighters heading out to sea blowing their fog horns. Kids playing ball on the grass. The bells from Saint John's Cathedral ringing every hour. Yeah, we like it there..Like to talk about the old days. We found a bench and sat down.

Phil: There were the good days, Herby.

Herby: Yeah, they were, Phil.

Phil: Some bad. Not many.

Herby: I remember one of the bad days.

Phil: Which one?

Herby: That day when you bought two Lotto tickets. One for you, and one for your dog Freddie.

Phil: You had to bring that up.

Herby: You gotta admit, Phil, bad day for you, but it is a funny story.

Phil: For you, maybe. Yeah, I remember that day. I buy two Lotto tickets. One for me and one for Freddie. We were partners. Anyway, a million to one shot. Freddie's ticket wins. Me and you, Freddie, we're rich! So what does Freddie do? He runs away from home with all the money. I never see him again. Last I heard he was living in Paris with a French Poodle.

Herby: I heard it said that a dog is man's best friend. Could be a story there, Phil.

Phil: No, hurts too much.

THE ROAD

BY BRETT HADLEY

Had I as many miles
To go
As I have already
Been;
Would I roll down that
Same old road,
Take the same old
Trip again?
This is not the downhill side,
It's not coasting through the day
The goal is not the end
But the sights along
The way.
And if I knew
That down that road
And just around the bend,
Lay all I have sought,
A world of delight,
Full of love and joy
And pleasure without end;

Should I not shun that turn,
And take the road to the right
Through the darkened tunnel,
Plunge into the night?
Yes, stick to the new trail
While the dream still burns;
Seek the unknown till the road ends,
And forego the places I have already been.

CHRISTMAS

BY DUKE ANDERSON

The first Christmas I can remember was when I was a tot in arms. I can recall my dad and mother holding me in their arms and letting me blow out the candles on the tree. This was before people strung electric lights all over their tree. Oh, the candles were so pretty.

The next Christmas I remember pretty well was when I was about five. The thing I wanted most in life was a steam engine. One that had a shovel and you could move shovels full of the earth. I was told that Santa Claus didn't have much money that year and not everybody could get what they wanted. And he had so many children. Maybe he couldn't remember every one. This happened when the Great Depression was just getting into full swing. My dad was working a part-time job at a Piggly-Wiggly Market in the produce section.

Earlier that afternoon, which was Christmas Eve, we had put up our Christmas tree. There were no presents under the tree, but the tree was so pretty. All the ornaments were so sparkly and colorful. That evening, after my supper Mother bundled me up and off we took to walk to the market to see my dad and walk him home. I had asked so many times if they thought Santa might remember me and what I had hoped for. They didn't say no, but they didn't say yes. We got to our street, finally to our apartment, and we walked up the stairway to our place. My dad opened the door. Mother, who had been holding my hand, let me in the door and there in front of the Christmas tree was the most beautiful, wonderful, brand new steam engine you ever saw. Oh, thank you, Santa! You remembered.

The next Christmas I remember was when I was about seven. We lived in an apartment in Hollywood, right up the street from the Hollywood Ranch Market on La Mirada Street.

I was in my bed, right next to a window. I was so excited because of Santa Claus that I couldn't go to sleep. I was supposed to be going to sleep, but I kept staring out the window, looking for Santa Claus and his sleigh. There were little puffy clouds in the sky, the moon was really bright, and I kept looking and hoping. What? What was that? I think. Yes! Yes! I can see Santa Claus and his reindeer and his sleigh, and they were going right across the sky in front of those puffy clouds. Santa Claus. "I saw him!" I yelled for my dad and mother. They raced into my room, wondering if I was okay. I yelled at them, even though they were right next to me and my bed. "I just saw Santa Claus and his sleigh. Right there." I pointed into the sky where I had seen him. I knew I would never forget that as long as I lived.

I remember other Christmas's too. The time I got my first two-wheel bike. The time I got my first basketball. And I remember the Christmas when I figured out who Santa Claus was.

And I remember the happiness and thrill it was when I became Santa Claus. I ended up with four of the sweetest, nicest, lovingest kids in the whole world. And I loved being Santa Claus and making as many of their dreams come true as was possible. They knew that Santa Claus could do miracles if you asked him nicely, and were good. They were all good, but one Christmas about two years ago, I found out that I would never see my youngest son at Christmas time again. And I couldn't make any miracles this time. This time when it really counted, I was helpless. I had had him to love for forty-four years. Forty-four years is such a short time. Especially if you love that person with all your heart. I held him in my arms when he was born. And I held his hand when he left us.

In my memory, Christmas has always been a time of fun and presents and joy and happiness with lots of love between family members and friends, too. But for the rest of my time, Christmas will always have a sad side to it for me, because I know there is no Santa Claus I can go to and ask for a gift I know he can't give.

I can give myself a gift though. A gift I can give myself is the huge amount of great memories I have stored up. I can open that Christmas gift any time of the year. Why not today? Merry Christmas, me.

DREAM

BY ANTHONY LAWRENCE

When darkling wash of night at last explodes,
And starry constellations silent shift,
My Gates of dreams divide the midnight roads,
Through ivory and horn to magic drift,
Beyond chaste thought and far from noxious fumes,
The warming globe, the hoi polloi, the beat,
I float mid ancient lochs and pink lagoons,
To coves where dandelion pearls smell sweet;
Then tender squalls sashay me through the stain,
Ascending up an incandescent sheen,
Where mystic creatures dance around my brain,
And peg-leg nonsense things cavort and preen:
Wood nymphs appear as dawn is set to break,
But shattered is my heart for now I wake.

AN EVENING'S MUSING

BY BRETT HADLEY

Alas, my friend,
Your sun will be setting soon.
You are standing on the edge of the
Great Hush.
The Dark Man stands
Quietly by.
How was your day?
How, in fact, were all
The days of your life?
And, what do you leave us
In your passing through?
A warm wind
Wafting by,
Or
A strident blast
To
Curse our day?
You do not go, my friend
Unseen, unheard, unknown, unloved
Though you may think so
But have you
Truly touched someone,
Put an imprint on
Any life, any soul?

Or
Have you just
Passed through like
Smoke on the wind?
You may well feel yourself
As
Ephemeral as smoke passing through,
But
Where you touch,
You cling,
Your being lingers;
Like it or not.

DEAR SON

BY SHELLEY BERMAN

Upon learning from his doctors that my son Joshua's life on Earth would be short, I wrote the following letter to him. I read it to him in Children's Hospital in Cincinnati in the last week of September 1977.

Since you are approaching thirteen—young manhood—and since you have been ill, I have decided to write you a letter of cheer. It is a letter, not a lesson, so if there are parts you do not understand it really doesn't matter. Whatever you think it means is correct. However, if anything here does not fill you with joy and pride and complete satisfaction, you have misunderstood it. Perhaps when you are older we will discuss this letter. Perhaps not. I would like your permission to let others know what I have written here because I am proud of it—not because I wrote it but because it says so much about you. There is no special reason for writing it at this time other than the fact that I am thinking these things right now—things I should have thought of before and regret I haven't—and I see no reason to wait and risk forgetting what I want to say.

In fact, even as I write, I seem to grow wings and fly through the sky and see you and the rest of the world from a point of view so vast and exciting I couldn't resist telling you about it even if I wanted to. And as I fly, my eyes become powerful beacons of light allowing me to see you better than ever. I know things about you now that I have never known before. And I begin to resent that parents are not naturally endowed with wings and bright eyes to always see their children as I see you at this moment. Suddenly I see you as you really are and have been for over twelve years. Until now

I have thought of you mostly as a young boy who must be prepared for his future. That's not wrong, of course. It is right for us to plan for your future. But what about now? What about all the "nows" you have already experienced, the "nows" I can share with you today? Have you any idea of all you have accomplished already? Do you have any notion of the number of things you've done, the gifts you've given, the goals you are attaining each new moment of your life?

Perhaps, my son, I am writing this letter to myself as well as to you. It is important for me to know these things, too. I want to adjust my thinking so I can better appreciate this young man I've been living with; this young man I am finally getting to know. Don't forget, Joshua, I am the man who has more than once called you "lazy."

Lazy? No word was ever more wrong in describing you. In fact you have shown me that perhaps parents ought to be prohibited by law from ever using that ugly word in front of their children. I'll tell you how "lazy" you've been: All the things you could ever hope to be you have already been. By this I mean if your ambition is to be a teacher, for example, or a great hero, you have already been these things. Truly you have been a teacher. I know because I have been one of your pupils. With patience and humor, you have instructed me in fatherhood; its wonders, joys and demands. Sometimes you were firm. Do you remember how you once scolded me when I apologized for not being a better father? What a lecture that was! You even taught me humor. I, a professional laugh-maker, have sat amazed at your gentle wit—your timely, tasteful humor, always appropriate, always exactly enough. You also taught me how to distinguish between important and unimportant. Through you I have learned to enjoy my work more and get along better with those around me. I was a slow learner, my young teacher, but I learned.

Are you also a hero? Yes. As your father I have given you much, but your courage is your own doing. You have endured pain. You have taken disappointment with grace and good cheer. You have faced up to fear and beaten it. What else must one do to be a hero? I have seen you try as hard as any man can try; seen you meet challenges I myself might have turned from and run. Your mother knows this about you. And your grandma, and your young sister. Your friends know it, and your teachers.

What else have you been? A poet, a painter of pictures, a thinker of deep thoughts, an ever-curious explorer of all around you. Heaven help us, you have even been a critic! Mostly you have been a person of sympathy and understanding. I know this because just as you are very selective in what you make jokes about, you are equally remarkable in what you choose to weep about. This is not to say it is wrong to weep about one's own pain or worry or disappointment. All people do this no matter how strong or wise they are. But I have seen you weep for the pain of others. And I have seen you weep for joy—the joy of others as well as your own. This, Joshua, is not a common kind of weeping, particularly for so young a man as yourself.

Do you recall the times when we have found ourselves sitting in silence looking into each other's eyes? We would look until our eyes brimmed with tears we could not explain. Those moments, I think, are among the most favorite moments of my life. Whatever we were saying to each other in those sweet silences was secret even to ourselves. But we knew, didn't we, that we were overcome by the fullness of our love and words had become unnecessary. You couldn't have been more than six the first time it happened—our eyes locking together until they overflowed. I was stunned by it. I was unable to describe it even to your mother. How hard you gazed! How steady were your fine, blue, innocent eyes. Such moments I know cannot be planned but I do look forward to more, many more of our tender silences.

Of course, Joshua, I am your father and I see your goodness more readily than I see the goodness of other young people. Yet I do not believe I am saying more about you than you deserve. I see you as a rarity. I see you as unique among all people, young and old. I see you not as a promise but as a fulfillment; not as something that will be, but as something that is. My son, you are not a problem to be solved, you are a result to be reckoned with as we reckon with the stars.

I see you now as more vast than space. I see you unbounded by so small a thing as time. These are strange words I am saying to you. Do not be bothered if I am being unclear. Though my words may be cloudy, my vision is clear, and what I know I know with absolute certainty, at least where you are concerned.

You are not in my presence as I write this, yet I am able to see you, feel your tight hug, hear your voice. And all the good of you surrounds me.

Remember our talks about infinity? Well, time and space are not the only things which are infinite. Good is infinite. Love is infinite. And, my son, in the universe as I know it, you are infinite.

I love you,

Daddy.

CONTRIBUTORS

RICHARD "DUKE" ANDERSON was raised in North Hollywood. He served in the U.S. Navy as a radio operator during World War II in the Pacific theater. Later he spent over thirty years working in radio, television, and movies, while raising his children Paul, Karen, Stacey, and Duke. He became a resident of MPTF in May 2013.

SHELLEY BERMAN was born in Chicago, Illinois. He was the first person to ever get a Grammy in 1959 for the first spoken word album. He was also the first comedian to ever play in Carnegie Hall. But Shelley Berman was much more than just a comedian and actor. He was a family man who adored his two children, Joshua and Rachel. Shelley spent many years volunteering at MPTF where his poetry class was very popular and well attended. In his later years, Shelley could still be seen on campus with his daughter Rachel, attending the Grey Quill Society to share his love for the written word.

WILLIAM BLINN was born in Toledo, Ohio. Bill attended the American Academy of Dramatic Arts. A prolific writer and producer, he created the series: *FAME, Our House, Starsky & Hutch, The New Land,* and *The Lazarus Syndrome,* among others. As well, Bill wrote many TV movies and mini-series including *Shane, A Man Called Intrepid, Brian's Song,* and the history-making *Roots.*

 SHIRLEY COHEN in her early years typed scripts for some of the great writers, beginning on Playhouse 90. Experiencing those words flow on the page seemed like it must be easy to write them but she tried it and found that it certainly is not easy. Not at all. Still, she enjoyed a world of inspiration being surrounded by those magical words in various stages of production behind the scenes for 50 years. Most rewarding was being Producer Walter Seltzer's assistant on some major films. Among them *Soylent Green*, *The Omega Man*, and *Will Penny*.

 ANNE FAULKNER: A true late bloomer. In Ohio: Metromedia executive in TV division, an actor and director in local theater wherever she lived. Mid-life: off to New York and Los Angeles becoming a full-time actor. Today: writer, actor, and mother of two, grandmother to seven, and great-grandmother to ten children.

 PHIL HABERMAN was born in the year 1925. Came to California in 1951 to find fame and fortune. Never found either one. Phil worked in the movie industry as a sound editor for forty-some-odd years. He's now a member of the Grey Quill Society. He's the one with the quills.

 ALFRED BRETT HADLEY is an actor who has performed in several movies, lots of TV shows, including eighteen years on *The Young and the Restless*, many TV commercials, and a great deal of live theater. Today he is focusing on writing life stories and finishing his novel.

LISABETH HUSH. New York City born and bred. Couldn't wait to get away. Had her SAG card and first job a few weeks after coming to LA. Became a for-life member of The Actors Studio, then Theatre West. Loves stage work, film, and TV. Poetry just started pouring from her in the '70s. Oh, yes, the more she learns of her family, she believes she's fulfilled all their hidden desires to act. Lucky Lisabeth.

DAVID KRAMER: After discharge from the United States Navy David was faced with the necessity of doing something other than attending classes and saluting. He chose film stardom. After bartending, cab driving and free-lancing his meager art skills for five years, and doing very, very little acting, he saw the writing on the wall. It said, "Press Release: Do entertainment publicity. It looked like fun and you get to dress swell and act important." I thought he could do that, and did for nearly fifty years, met a lot of nifty people, married twice, and sired two great kids.

ANTHONY LAWRENCE was a prolific TV writer who also co-wrote three Elvis Presley films, then wrote and produced a three-hour Presley biopic. Tony has received four WGA nominations and is on the Writers' Guild list of 101 best-written TV series for *Gunsmoke*, *Columbo*, and *The Fugitive*.

MAGGIE MALOOLY was born in Chicago, Illinois. Relocating to Los Angeles, she has appeared in more than three hundred TV commercials, twenty-six roles on various TV series, and hosted morning talk shows. Maggie has produced, written, and hosted TV and radio travel segments, and produced three live appearances of Rock Hudson in Argentina and Brazil. Her most cherished and treasured production: four children and four grandchildren.

MICHAEL REAVES is an Emmy Award-winning television writer and screenwriter whose many credits include *Star Trek: The Next Generation, Twilight Zone, Batman: The Animated Series*; and *Gargoyles*. His novels include the *New York Times* bestseller *Darth Maul: Shadow Hunter* and the forthcoming *Star Wars: Death Star*.

JOEL ROGOSIN is a veteran Hollywood "hyphenate"—a writer/producer/director—with over thirty years of experience in the entertainment industry, and perhaps hundreds of credits on primetime TV series and movies. On two occasions he also produced *The Jerry Lewis Labor Day Telethon*—twenty-one live hours—for the Muscular Dystrophy Association. He has written screenplays, poetry, two produced stage musicals, and a published memoir, *Writing a Life*, and conducts innovative writing workshops, The Creative Adventure, in various nationwide venues. He and his wife, Deborah, a marriage and family therapist, have three daughters and five grandchildren and are looking forward to their first great-grandson.

DEBORAH ROGOSIN was born and raised in California. She lived around the corner from her future husband, Joel Rogosin, and started dating him when she was eighteen. After two years of college, she married Joel and dropped out of school in order to support him during his last year at Stanford. They moved to LA after college and started a family—three daughters in five years—while Joel broke into showbiz. Deborah returned to her studies, pursuing a masters degree in art when she developed retinitis pigmetosa, a genetic condition that led to her gradual loss of sight. Undeterred, she pursued a degree in psychology and has been a licensed psychotherapist for thirty-six years.

ALAN SLOAN began his career in the industry in the mailroom at ABC in 1954. He worked at Ted Bates advertising as a media Buyer and then as a salesman at CBS. In 1963 under their auspices he took mid-career break earning a Ph.D. in political behavior at M.I.T. doing his field work in Peru. Upon returning to CBS he eventually became VP, General Manager of WCBS-TV. In 1970, with his wife and three children, he left NY for Hollywood where he worked as a company executive as well as an independent producer-writer on numerous television movies and series. He retired to Florida in 1999 where he became active in Senior issues. He returned to California in 2015 and is currently serving on the Executive Council of AARP California.

MADI SMITH-LAWRENCE was a concert violinist and dancer, although not at the same time. She has worked in the entertainment business for over forty-five years. She received her AF of M, AFTRA, and SAG cards in 1954 when she was put under contract to Paramount. She worked at NBC for ten years as a scheduler in broadcast operations and control, and as liaison between NBC and the Directors Guild of America. Following her years at NBC, Madi worked as an executive assistant for the Smothers Brothers, Bobby Darin, Danny Arnold, and Norman Lear, among others.

JOAN TANNEN was born in White Plains, New York. She has been a resident at the MPTF for close to twelve years. She was a secretary at Screen Gems, the Directors Guild of American, and CBS. Joan's husband, Charles, was an actor under contract to 20th Century Fox and continued acting until 1963 when he became a television comedy writer. In addition to her writing, Joan enjoys oil painting, Wii golf, and bowling, and improv, and writes and produces for Chanel 22 and the *Resident Gazette*.

 KAY WEISSMAN: My birth certificate says Wilma Kay Friedman, born 1936, Detroit, Michigan. I changed my name to Antonia Flores when I became a Spanish dancer and performed with Jose Greco throughout Europe at seventeen. Then got my SAG card as Kay Freeman in 1973, to be a bridesmaid in *The Godfather*. There were many names and performances in between, studying with Uta Hagan, Herbert Berghoff, Charles Nelson Reilly, Warren Robertson, and every actor and director I ever worked with. My greatest joy came in 1996 when I married Murray Weissman, P.R. executive and became, Mrs. Murray Weissman!!!

GRATITUDE

The Grey Quill Society owes a debt of gratitude to the many women and men whose support has made this publication possible. Countless fellow members of the entertainment community, MPTF employees, volunteers, and campus residents continually work behind the scenes to provide us with the services, facilities, and most importantly encouragement to pursue out writing efforts every week.

Our heartfelt thanks to:

The California Writers Club San Fernando Branch for their generous artistic and financial support.

Morrison Senior Services for providing the coffee and pastries that fuel our workshops every Thursday morning, without which we would face serious writer's block.

Rachel Berman and Ben Cowitt, tireless Grey Quill Society volunteers, for their ability to tackle any task asked of them with enthusiasm and humor.

Our editorial board: Victoria Bullock, Brent Thomas, and David Kramer for their literary rigor and wisdom.

Karen Richardson for the gift of artistry that became her cover-to-cover design, and the hundreds of hours she spent making it look easy as she made us look good.

Ed Stauss for his essential but often overlooked and underappreciated copy editing.

Additionally, we thank heaven for loaning us Shelley Berman and David Kramer even as we cope with the sadness of losing these two dear friends and fine writers, both of whom are represented in this collection. While they were with us we were blessed by their wit, their insight, and their humanity. Neither man could have been more important to us, or more loved. They are with us, still, every Thursday.

And finally:

It's been said before, but we'll say it again: Quality in any organization starts at the top, and we couldn't be more fortunate to have as our fearless leader and staunchest advocate Bob Beitcher. As President and CEO of The Motion Picture and Television Fund, Bob oversees what many regard as the finest, non-profit, all-inclusive wellness and retirement community maybe in the universe. This doesn't happen by luck or mistake. It happens because one person, one huge heart, can make a difference. Our gratitude for that inspiration cannot be overstated.

—Ed.

Made in the USA
San Bernardino, CA
17 December 2018